ORIGIN *of* MY BIRTHPLACE

ORIGIN *of* MY BIRTHPLACE

Knowing God and
Connecting to the Source of Life

JOHN
BLACKWELL

NEW YORK

ORIGIN *of* MY BIRTHPLACE
Knowing God and Connecting to the Source of Life

Published in New York, New York, by Morgan James Publishing. Morgan James and The Entrepreneurial Publisher are trademarks of Morgan James, LLC.
www.MorganJamesPublishing.com

The Morgan James Speakers Group can bring authors to your live event. For more information or to book an event visit The Morgan James Speakers Group at www.TheMorganJamesSpeakersGroup.com.

A FREE eBook edition is available
with the purchase of this print book

CLEARLY PRINT YOUR NAME IN THE BOX ABOVE

Instructions to claim your free eBook edition:
1. Download the BitLit app for Android or iOS
2. Write your name in UPPER CASE in the box
3. Use the BitLit app to submit a photo
4. Download your eBook to any device

ISBN 978-1-63047-162-0 paperback
ISBN 978-1-63047-163-7 eBook
ISBN 978-1-63047-164-4 hardcover
Library of Congress Control Number:
2014933881

Cover Design by:
Rachel Lopez
www.r2cdesign.com

Interior Design by:
Bonnie Bushman
bonnie@caboodlegraphics.com .

In an effort to support local communities, raise awareness and funds, Morgan James Publishing donates a percentage of all book sales for the life of each book to Habitat for Humanity Peninsula and Greater Williamsburg.

Get involved today, visit
www.MorganJamesBuilds.com.

Habitat
for Humanity®
Peninsula and
Greater Williamsburg
Building Partner

To Philip P. Kerstetter
Mentor and Friend
With Gratitude

CONTENTS

The Dreams	1
Learning to See	5
Deep Calling Unto Deep	8
Involvement and Insight	14
The Palpable Draw	21
The Cathedral, the World, and Experience	28
Knowing Each Other at our Best	32
Recognizing the Voice	38
Curiosity	41
From Curiosity to Mystery	45
The Expanse	50
The Genesis Altar	54
The Altar, the Expanse, and the Image of God	60
Matrix of Creativity	64
Communion with the Expanse	70
Abram's Knowing	76
The Key Window	82
The Faith of Abraham	88
Leonardo's Virgin of the Rocks	99
The North Windows	105

Insight from Mark   110
Insight from Luke   121
Insight from John   134
Insight from Matthew   142
The Origin of My Birthplace   154
The Labyrinth   163

Appendix   *167*
Obstacles to Primary Knowing   *168*
Paths to Primary Knowing   *173*
Acknowledgments   *180*
About the Author   *182*
Books by John Blackwell   *183*

The free man is he who wills without arbitrary self-will.

He believes in destiny, and believes that it stands in need of him. It does not keep him in leading-strings, it awaits him, he must go to it, yet does not know where it is to be found. But he knows that he must go out with his whole being. The matter will not turn out according to his decision; but what is to come will come only when he decides on what he is able to will. He must sacrifice his puny, unfree will, that is controlled by things and instincts, to his grand will, which quits defined for destined being. Then, he intervenes no more, but at the same time he does not let things merely happen. He listens to what is emerging from himself, to the course of being in the world; not in order to be supported by it, but in order to bring it to reality as it desires.

—**Martin Buber,** *I and Thou*

You must close the eyes and call instead upon another vision which is to be waked within you, a vision which all possess, which few apply.

—**Plotinus,** *Enneads*

THE DREAMS

God is also in sleep, and Dreams advise,
Which he hath sent propitious, some great good
Presaging
—Eve, in John Milton, *Paradise Lost*

Dreams are often the doorways into these other worlds. When a great dream occurs it does not make much sense to look at the individual happenings of a person's life; rather, it is understood to be a message from a reality that lies outside the normal limits of our senses.

—David Peat, *Blackfoot Physics*

The dream could not have been more clear. The color blue embodied the smog-free sky. I was above the ocean, in the center of which was a hole that was penetrated by breath, pure white in color. The breath blew in a straight line over the sky-blue ocean, rising slightly as it approached the center. It rose because the waters surrounding the center rose as well, forming a gentle, raised circle that surrounded the center, causing the waters to slope gently towards the center, where the pure white breath penetrated the waters. Lines of white breath sloped gently over the surface of the raised circle, also moving towards the center. But the single line of breath which blew over the waters, rising and then shooting straight down with complete, decisive deliberation, dominated all other movements of breath.

This clear vision in the dream came to me as a single image immediately prior to waking. Some dreams are clear and compelling. This was one of them. When I awoke, I knew in the core of my being that I had been given a gift—this dream. The gift was not something that I had earned. There was nothing good or meritorious in me that made me uniquely eligible for the dream; nor did the dream in any way exalt me or make me a better person. It was the fact that there was nothing meritorious in me that constituted the dream as a gift. It was not a gift to be taken lightly or squandered. This dream was to be treasured—pondered, reflected, understood, acted on, and then pondered again, and yet again. The dream bore the first fruits of primary knowing—a kind of knowing that is direct, in which the knower and the known are in a mutually rewarding symbiotic communion.

The image carried a surplus of ambiguity. It embodied the capacity to receive, bear, and re-generate circumstances, connections, relationships, understanding, interactions, and thinking itself. I can understand that some people will struggle with ambiguity. There are times when all of us crave simple, easy answers. I've come to understand that ambiguity can be a great gift. An image from a dream or literature or a painting that is teeming with ambiguity creates in our imaginations a capacity for rich, direct knowing and deep understanding. An image that is fraught with ambiguity is neither limited nor limiting. An image rich in ambiguity provides us with the opportunity to bring our own circumstances, thinking, and action to bear. The ambiguous image becomes a substantive source of transformation and generativity.

The image in my dream was both silent and fertile: its meaning would unfold without effort or exhaustion. The discovery of one meaning would give birth to a communion of meaning that is ever ripe in the unfolding of mystery and discovery.

On the morning of this dream, I was aware that the bright sky-blue ocean of the dream was the deep of my own soul. Equally clear was that the breath that blew over the waters of my soul was the breath of God, which penetrated the center of my being with complete decisiveness. The breath of God went straight into the core of my most true self and was intimately involved with both consciousness and my greater unconscious. Because of the penetrating presence of the breath of God, consciousness and my unconscious formed a creative whole. The connection of consciousness and the unconscious are essential to this creativity. The breath of God was enlivening me from without, forming an inter-connection with inner connections. So enlivening was this interconnection that at the time that was ripe, a well of living water gushed forth from the center of my soul. The dream became a reality of wonder.

This first dream offered a primary image to be observed and understood in a knowing silence. It was complemented by a second dream that when coupled with the first dream constituted the generating origin of my soul. The second dream was pure voice. There was no image, nothing to see. The quality of the voice was rich, husky, and deep—at once firm and kind: *I keep taking something fresh to the origin of my birthplace.*

The gift of the two dreams presented to my consciousness the opportunity to know, to understand, and to participate in the origin of my soul. The dreams came to me at two different, but complementary times. With them came an intuition—that when I connected these two dreams as an act of imagination, the connection brought me to the origin of my soul. These words were a description of both the way I am to live and a knowing that is primary—direct and completely involved. Their connection is essential; it forms an inner, spiritual, generating whole. My connecting with the origin of my birthplace is a matter of both my responsibility and my will.

As I spent time reflecting on the two dreams, I understood that my birthplace has an origin, a source. This origin is not so much to be located in time and space, but to be identified and known—in acts of conscious willingness. It is also clear that this essentiality is an ever-present generating principle. I am to be aware of it; I am to know it; and I am to bring the world in which I have direct interaction to it. This is my calling; this is my responsibility; this is the reason for my life.

The two dreams are linked in an insight: they are two halves of a reality that is complete in their interconnection. The words, "I keep taking something fresh to the origin of my birthplace," are the verbal complement to the image of the pure white breath of God blowing over the sky-blue ocean of my being and penetrating deep into the center, where it creates an expanse of light, life, and generativity. I learned that it is my responsibility to know the essential connection between these two dreams and the communion to which they give birth. It is my calling to take something fresh to the origin of my birthplace. This image is the origin of my birthplace. It is the inner place to which I can take the substance of life and connect it with creativity and generativity.

LEARNING TO SEE

Be not afeard; the isle is full of noises,
Sounds and sweet airs, that give delight and hurt not.
Sometimes a thousand twangling instruments
Will hum about mine ears, and sometime voices
That, if I then had waked after long sleep,
Will make me sleep again: and then, in dreaming,
The clouds methought would open and show riches
Ready to drop upon me that, when I waked,
I cried to dream again.
—William Shakespeare, *The Tempest*

All knowledge has its origin in our perceptions.
—Leonardo da Vinci

I f I have learned anything in life, I have learned the importance
of learning to see. I have also learned that learning to see takes
time. In my case, it takes far more time than I would ever wish. I
am not burdened with patience, and I can be critically impatient with

myself. There are times I think myself the world's slowest learner and latest bloomer.

The figure who convinced me of the importance of learning to see was the Italian Renaissance artist Leonardo (1452–1519). For him, learning to see was everything. His skill as an artist was founded on his ability to see. Leonardo had the remarkable ability to see whatever was in front of him. When I started reading Leonardo's biography, or looking at his astonishing paintings, I realized how completely underdeveloped was my ability to see. Leonardo was a genius in many respects, all of which seem to be founded on his uncanny ability actually to see.

There is a second genius who made an important impact on my understanding of the importance of learning to see, and that was Mark. In the eighth chapter, Mark has the first of his two stories of the Healing of the Blind Man. The story is as peculiar as it is straightforward. Some people brought a blind man to Jesus and begged Jesus to touch the man. Jesus removed the blind man from the crowd, after which he spit on his eyes. Jesus then asked the man if he could see. The man reported that he could see people, but they looked like trees walking. Jesus then touched the man's eyes. He was finally able to see everything with clarity.

There is much to observe in this story, and the observations are all important. One of the things we notice is that the first two interactions between the man and Jesus (taking the man away from other people and spitting on his eyes) did not produce the effect of clear eyesight. A third interaction was necessary. Among other things Mark shows us is that learning to see takes time.

I begin with these insights from Leonardo and Mark for two reasons. The first is that my own learning to see has taken an enormous amount of time. There have been occasions when my learning has been painfully slow. I wish I were a quicker study. I have nothing but admiration for those who are blessed with seemingly effortless insight— especially when it comes to recognizing the most important things that are emerging. The second is that great literature, including the Bible, is about learning to see. This is especially true with the Gospels and the book of Genesis. Among other things, these important books involve learning to recognize the presence of God and what is emerging and unfolding in the world.

The reason I begin with a word about the development of my own observational abilities is that a friend, Ryan Fields, who looked at the first draft of my manuscript, asked me about the order of the essays I have written. I told Ryan that I have tried to make each essay stand on its own so that it could be read and understood by itself. The editor Roy Carlisle taught me that today's reader wants to be able to open a book and start anywhere, picking and choosing as she goes. This means that it is important that each essay be complete. I have tried to heed Roy's wisdom. I then shared with Ryan that the order of the essays reflects ways in which my own thinking and observational abilities have developed over the years. Another way to put this is that the order of the essays reflects the ways things have emerged in my own imagination.

When I started reading the American author Flannery O'Connor (first her stories and novels, and then her essays), I began to realize that she was not only bearing witness to what she was seeing, including the unfolding of the presence and power of God, but she was also giving her readers the eyes with which to recognize the emerging and unfolding of presence and meaning in our lives. At the time I was reading Flannery O'Connor, I also started reading Joseph Jaworski, who was writing about the predictable miracles that were unfolding in his life. This strengthened my desire and determination to be able to answer the question, how do I recognize the presence of the power of God, including what is emerging and unfolding? How do I learn to see? And how does my ability to see lead to understanding and knowing what is authentic and direct?

What follows is one result of my effort to see and to understand what is emerging right before our eyes.

DEEP CALLING
UNTO DEEP

*Things of importance come to me not in philosophical reflections,
but in flashes, in sudden perceptions of the unseen, indeed I suppose
I must say in visions. It is not, I assure you, because I have a screw
loose, but because my arrangement of screws is wholly personal.*
        —Robertson Davies, "The Novelist and Magic"

You can observe a lot by watching.

                                                —Yogi Berra

When it came to a sense of wonder and mystery, my maternal grandmother, Leta, was a great influence. One of my earliest memories of her influence involved a circle meeting of twelve or so women in my grandmother's living room. At the end of the meeting, the women joined hands in a circle to pray. I was included. As I listened to their prayer, I heard them say, "And Leta is not in temptation." This is my earliest memory of The Lord's Prayer.

The following Sunday, my grandmother took me to Asbury Methodist Church in San Diego. I sat with one of her friends because my grandmother sang in the choir, which processed down the center aisle at the beginning of the service. I will never forget how much I held the procession in awe: my grandmother was at the front of the line. Every kindergartener knows that when the teacher tells the class to line up, there is a rush to be first—at the head of the line. When I saw my grandmother at the head of the line in her choir robe, I knew that she and church were special. Later in the service, my understanding was confirmed during the time of prayer. I heard the whole congregation pray—out loud!—"And Leta is not in temptation!"

I loved my grandmother. She was special. She made me feel special. And she carried about her a great sense of something that I would later come to understand as wonder, mystery, and the numinous. There were times in my life that I buried or ignored mystery, but it never left me. There were also times when it was clear that there was something on the inside that sought a Something on the Outside. I would finally learn that to ignore that Something was at best to short-change my life. Worse, I discovered that when we ignore the numinous and mystery, we needlessly place our lives at peril.

Robertson Davies was once giving a lecture in a university. He was sharing experiences that were deeply personal. They had everything to do with who he was not only as a writer, but also as a human being. This included his experience of the "numinous." (Davies did not like the term "supernatural.") He also talked about the kinds of ideas that came to him, seemingly out of nowhere. Important insights came to Davies as visions. Because he was giving this talk to a highly educated audience, Davies anticipated the skepticism with which his lecture would be met. I find his words to be refreshing and disarming. To give an accounting of the reason and way that ideas came to him, he told his audience, "It is not, I assure you, because I have a screw loose, but because my arrangement of screws is wholly personal."

From time to time I will find myself identifying with a statement or an entire outlook of one of Robertson Davies's characters. When I read his autobiographical statement, "my arrangement of screws is wholly personal," I felt as though Davies were talking about the hard wiring in my brain. I am sure there are many people—not only enemy, but also friend—who would say of me, "He has a screw loose." Although I wouldn't entirely blame someone for having that kind of opinion of me, I do find, like Davies, that the arrangement of screws in my mind is wholly personal. There are ways of looking at the world, insights and experiences with which I not only resonate but do so completely. The circuitry of the Blackwell brain has a lot to say about the kinds of things that interest me.

One of the books that interest me greatly is William James's *Varieties of Religious Experience*. The book consists of the Gifford Lectures that James gave in Edinburgh in 1900. During the same time that Sigmund Freud was writing and lecturing about the unconscious, James was writing and lecturing about people's experiences of God. One of the things I respect about William James is that he allows the experiences to speak for themselves. One that I find particularly compelling comes near the beginning of the book. A man writes:

> I remember the night, and almost the very spot on the hill-top, where my soul opened out, as it were, into the Infinite, and there was a rushing together of the two worlds, the inner and the outer. It was deep calling unto deep—the deep that my own struggle had opened up within being answered by the unfathomable deep without, reaching beyond the stars. I stood alone with Him who had made me, and all the beauty of the world, and love, and sorrow, and even temptation. I did not seek Him, but felt the perfect unison of my spirit with His. The ordinary sense of things around me faded. For the moment nothing but an ineffable joy and exultation remained. It is

impossible fully to describe the experience. It was like the effect of some great orchestra when all the separate notes have melted into one swelling harmony that leaves the listener conscious of nothing save that his soul is being wafted upwards, and almost bursting with its own emotion.

The perfect stillness of the night was thrilled by a more solemn silence. The darkness held a presence that was all the more felt because it was not seen. I could not any more have doubted that HE was there than that I was. Indeed, I felt myself to be, if possible, the less real of the two.

There are many things I find remarkable about this report. To begin, the man reports his experience directly without a lot of interpretation. He doesn't describe or defend his experience with theological categories or doctrinal positions. He isn't trying to justify his experience; he simply describes what happened. It is clear from his report that this experience or vision came, as it were, "out of nowhere." It seems not to have been contrived or fabricated. The man seems almost completely surprised by the encounter. It was, in other words, unsought, spontaneous, and involuntary.

Perhaps most striking are the interconnections that the man reports. He experienced a "rushing together of two worlds—inner and outer." The man recognized that the two worlds are distinct. One world—his inner world—is completely personal and is characterized by struggle. The man's inner world is clearly answered from without. Somehow, his own experience is connected "beyond the stars." His inner world develops an identity with the outer world. The harmony between these two worlds is so complete that he senses a "unison" between his own spirit and the spirit of God. His encounter with mystery is self-evident. Darkness holds a presence. The presence involves a connection between his own life, which is incomplete and still unfolding, and a reality that is as complete as it is real. This man's experience is wholly personal and self-evident. He was possessed by a knowing—that at that time, he was connected to both God and mystery.

There are several things that William James seeks to accomplish in his reports of people's experiences of God. James allows people's experiences to speak for themselves. He allows for people's experiences to be wholly personal. James takes care not to try to fit another person's experience into his own personal mold. He doesn't have a theory or formula that he is trying to validate. He isn't looking to defend his own religious position or ideas. Instead, James reports other people's primary experience.

Equally important is the fact that the people whom James studied are in many respects ordinary. They are not role models or super stars. All of the people James writes about struggle with life, and many fail to fit the norms that are shared in common culture:

> Often they have led a discordant inner life, and had melancholy during a part of their career. They have known no measure, been liable to obsessions and fixed ideas; and frequently they have fallen into trances, heard voices, seen visions, and presented all sorts of peculiarities which are ordinarily classed as pathological.

Perhaps most important is that we can see in William James's subjects a quality of incompleteness. They are not people who are omni-competent. These are human beings who are unfinished. Why do I find this to be important? People who by their own admission "have it all together" are not, I think, the kind of people who will be open to either the numinous or to God. If I think of myself as complete and finished, then I will have little, if any, room for another form of completeness in my life. Instead, I will tend to think of experiences that are qualitatively different from my own self-defined completeness as intrusive and perhaps threatening. To put it another way, it may be that a person's awareness of his or her own incompleteness and personal shortcomings is necessary for openness to and recognition of the numinous, God, or the order and wholeness of the world. If nothing else, the experience that William James describes involves a coming together of the complete with the incomplete—a rushing together of two different worlds, the meeting of which presents the possibility of a new kind of whole.

INVOLVEMENT
AND INSIGHT

Treasure this ecstasy, however senseless it may seem to men. My friends, pray to God for gladness. Be glad as children, as the birds of heaven.

—Father Zossima in Fyodor Dostoevsky,
The Brothers Karamazov

I can't pinpoint a particular moment when I first wanted to know the deep and the numinous. I can, however, remember significant moments along the way when I felt the nudge or urge to begin to understand and make sense of things that were stirring in my heart and imagination. As I continued to try to grow (this was never easy), I found myself, more and more, wanting to open my life to The Infinite. I found myself possessed by the numinous feeling that this was what I was supposed to do, and that were I to fail to do so, I would squander the chance, the life that had been given to me as a gift.

This began to happen in concert with people I met and authors I read. Paula D'Arcy was one. Her experience of and interaction with God are realities I have pondered for over twenty years. I am still captivated by her experience and anticipate that I always shall be. Paula was the first person who called my attention to the Cathedral of Chartres in France, especially its famous Labyrinth. When I was with Paula— listening to her speak to groups, or in personal conversation—I found myself resonating with her experience of God, which I also found to be self-authenticating and wholly real. Something inside me said that a pathway and a direction were opening.

It wasn't long after I met Paula that I began reading Joseph Jaworski. Not only were predictable miracles unfolding in his life, but he also found a mesmerizing resonance with the Cathedral of Chartres. Jaworski found the presence of a palpable mystery in the Cathedral that was somehow connected to the presence of the entire universe. The words of Paula D'Arcy and Joseph Jaworski drew me to the Cathedral. There, I discovered a whole world in which I could draw insight and meaning. It was a world of marvel. I began not only studying and pondering the Cathedral, but also recognizing vibrant connections to books I was reading that captivated me for their stunning insight.

My reading included Fyodor Dostoevsky, Flannery O'Connor, Homer, Dante, William Shakespeare, William James, Joseph Jaworski, David Bohm, Paula D'Arcy, and Robertson Davies. I spent lots of time in the books of Genesis and the four Gospels. Slowly, I began to see that each of these writers embodied, or led to, a kind of knowing that was primary. I have Mr. Jaworski to thank for the phrase, "primary knowing," which I read and re-read in his book, *Source*. Jaworski got his insight into primary knowing from Eleanor Rosch.

I found myself captivated and mesmerized by the idea and possibility of primary knowing. How do I describe it? The easiest might be to contrast primary knowing with secondary knowledge. Secondary knowledge involves knowing *about* someone or something. *Knowledge* is a noun. It is more or less fixed and settled. *Knowing* is a verb. It is active, involved, and direct. It is one thing, for example, for me to have knowledge about people; it is another to know them directly. Primary knowing involves knowing both God and the order of the world directly. I can't imagine anything more important.

Rosch and Jaworski found that the path to primary knowing begins with sustained observation. To know in a primary way, we have to stick with it, taking all the time that knowing requires. When we give our full, sustained, open attention to something of great import, eventually our sustained observing deepens into primary knowing that is direct and completely involved. Primary knowing becomes complete when we then, somehow, act on the fruits of primary knowing. In this way, our primary knowing begins to stay with us and to transform us from the inside.

What Mr. Jaworski discovered in his experience was that his willingness to observe led to a primary knowing that took him to the Source—the origin and matrix of all of life. As I poured over his book, *Source*, I was mesmerized by the connection between what Jaworski was discovering to unfold in his life with what I was reading in Genesis 1, particularly the second and fourth days of creation. I also noticed that Genesis 1 is about the formatting of the world and that this story also makes it possible for us to format our own experience, to the end that we can live in communion with one another, with God, and with the order of the universe.

As Jaworski shared his experience, he made it clear that there was nothing special about him as a person that made primary knowing possible. In other words, primary knowing is not dependant on special gifts, charisma, or talent. Primary knowing is not esoteric and accessible only to the initiated elite. Instead, primary knowing involves the willingness to explore vital connections between our lives, the unfolding order of the universe, and God.

I found this to be encouraging. If Jaworski was right, anyone could pursue knowing God, the unseen interconnections of the universe, and communion—including me.

As I read the important authors I mentioned above, there were two matters that caught my attention. The first was that none of them involved heavy theory. Instead, all of them shared a kind of experience with God and with the interconnections of the world that was both direct and refreshing. I still find the experiences that their writing embodies to be astonishing. These are writings with which I become completely involved. The second was that these writings themselves began to draw my imagination into an experience of knowing that was direct, compelling, and self-authenticating. Again, it was necessary to invest large blocks of time and to stick with it. These authors didn't write text messages. Their composition draws me in because it is of the finest comprehensive quality and is about matters of breath-giving import.

Slowly (and this took years), I began to discover that primary knowing is the fruit of willingly involving ourselves with God and the emerging and unfolding order of the universe. The place to begin is right where we are. That is the only place to begin; there is no other place. For me, one important point of entry was the writing of Fyodor Dostoevsky. In his masterpiece, *The Brothers Karamazov*, Father Zossima, the saintly Russian monk, urges people to regard prayer as a great education. An education in prayer involves loving every person, every creature, and every element of God's creation. Father Zossima recognizes that learning to love with consistency is never easy. Learning to persevere in love involves actively mobilizing everything that is good in the human spirit and being vigilant with reference to internal roadblocks and threats to love.

Brother Lawrence, a seventeenth century monk whose insight and practice of love is also of great value to me, recognized the importance of not beating up on ourselves when we fail to love or don't make the progress that we wish. He found it essential that we take steps to get ourselves back on track—immediately, quietly, and without fanfare. Both Father Zossima and Brother Lawrence teach us that learning to be present to the love of God with consistency is a dearly purchased treasure. At the same time, no one else can do it for us. Knowing God and knowing God's world in a primary way require both time and total commitment.

One of the reasons I have found Father Zossima and Brother Lawrence to be so important is that they don't rely on formulae or theories. They are interested in our engaging God, one another, and the world directly. This has been important to me because developing and applying theory is one of the things I have been best at. When I was in seminary and graduate school, theory was my strong suit. I loved it. I loved coming up with theoretical constructs that explained ideas and data in multiple contexts. My problem was that I used my theories to analyze just about everything, including people, whom I would then hold hostage not only to my theories about life, but also to my ways of thinking. Eventually, my theories and formulae became so real in my own mind that they became substitutes for God and for life itself. Instead of seeking to know God as God wants to be known, I relished *my* explanations of God and theories about God. Worse, I sometimes tried to use my facility with theories and formulae to establish my own superiority. At the same time, I used my theories to measure anyone and anything I deemed as the fair target of my theory, and far more often than not, found them wanting. I was just that arrogant.

And yet, when I read the words of Father Zossima or Brother Lawrence or Joseph Jaworski or Paula D'Arcy, I noticed several things. First, these figures do not use theory as a substitute for engaging God, people, and reality directly. They are thoughtful, to be sure. But they are far more engaged in doing and understanding than they are in theorizing and explaining. They are interested in primary experience, and they convey experience in ways that we, too, can jump in and participate—not to replicate their experience, but to live with our own knowing and authenticity. They recognize this kind of experience and involvement as essential to both our humanity and to our connections to one another and the world.

Father Zossima and Brother Lawrence filled my imagination, and my imagination then told me that I needed to make experience with God and the unfolding order of the world my own. Simply to replicate the experience of others was secondary. I needed to learn to love; I needed to learn to be in communion with people and the world. For me, imagination is critical, and it is essential that I continue to fill my imagination with some of what is best in the world. I found some of what is best in the Cathedral of Chartres. There, I discovered a world that is whole—a world where each part is essential to a miraculous whole. In a word, I found a world complete in its interconnections. Once that insight had me, I felt compelled to explore connections between the Cathedral, what I was reading, and the life I was trying to learn to live.

One of the most important things I had to learn was that seeing connections and living in an interconnected world of love was my responsibility. I couldn't clone, or replicate, the experience of others. I had to take their experience and then meet the Presence of God with my own willingness, imagination, and interaction. I had to learn the paradox that communion is a gift for which I am responsible.

The essays that follow are the partial embodiment of my experience with the insight to which primary knowing gives birth. On the one hand, I in no way want to hold myself as a role model. There are times when I struggle, get discouraged, and wonder if I will ever become the person that at the core of my being I know I should become. There are other times when I know for sure that I have been created for the kinds of connections that others have discovered. Still, this isn't an autobiography or a memoire. It is my effort to share something of the interconnections that I was able to discover in my knowing. I share it because, as Jaworski showed me, if I can do it, anyone can. That being said, I have learned that I have to make this experience my own, and others can do the same.

I would love for my insights to serve as a door through which others can gain their own insight. I find that there is nothing as important as learning to interact with God, people, and the emerging order of the world. This is the great adventure. It is also a dream that is completely possible. Just as I found the source of this insight in dreams, I also found it in the Cathedral of Chartres.

THE PALPABLE DRAW

As I was there, I experienced the most unusual feeling, a sort of ringing in my ears and entire head. It's difficult for me to describe, but it was distinctly familiar. It was as if I were in a different energy field altogether. I had experienced that feeling many times out in the wilderness, but this was the first time it had happened to me in a structure built by human hands.

—Joseph Jaworski, *Synchronicity*

Something mysterious was unfolding. It was remarkable and compelling. There was something about the Cathedral of Chartres that resonated with Joseph Jaworski. He describes the feeling as unusual—"a sort of ringing in my ears and entire head." The Cathedral was somehow tuning his mind and his entire being into a reality that was nothing short of a wonder. In some sense, Joseph Jaworski found himself to be connected to realities that are both eternal and unfolding. He also found that what he was experiencing in the Cathedral was connected to discoveries that he was making in the rest of his life. Somehow, it all came together in the Cathedral of Chartres.

21

Somehow, this Cathedral embodied the mystery that Jaworski was beginning to discover.

The first time I entered the Cathedral, the sense of mystery was palpable. It was also clear that I not only did not understand the mystery, but it would take years for things to come to an adequate measure of satisfying insight. And even when I began to understand matters that were important, there were always additional matters to explore. I sensed that there was much that I *could* understand, given ample time for observation and reflection. When I entered the Cathedral for the first time, I couldn't help but enjoy the aliveness with which the cathedral seemed to reverberate. The sensation reminded me of a line from James Joyce's *Portrait of the Artist as a Young Man*, which involves "the luminous silent stasis of aesthetic pleasure." The sensation was clearly one of pleasure. The pleasure was at once numinous and luminous. It was a pleasure that somehow fit both body and mind. The joy and bliss were quietly compelling. This was not a bliss that was fleeting or trivial; it was self authenticating. It reverberated with what Claude Tresmontant calls the "mystery of delectation." The mysteries were present for me to recognize, explore, and to savor. Mystery was connected to mystery, creating yet greater mystery which we can savor, understand, and treasure.

Chartres is in France, an hour by train south (and a little to the west) of Paris. Two things drew me to the Cathedral. One was the famous labyrinth on the floor of the nave. I had read about it, heard about it, and wanted to know something about why this particular labyrinth was a draw to so many people. The other was a book by Joseph Jaworski, entitled *Synchronicity*. In this book, Jaworski describes the discoveries that he was making that were somehow connected with the Cathedral. Jaworski writes about an unseen, but clearly embodied and perceptible, order of the universe. It is an order that is self-evident for those who are willing to participate in it. This order unfolds in the lives of people, communities, and events. It is also embodied in great art. When we are aware of and give attention to this order, remarkable, subtle, and sometimes astonishing events unfold. Events that might otherwise seem coincidences are what Jaworski calls "predictable miracles." It was clear from the quality of Jaworski's writing that his subject matter and experience were authentic. His excellence of composition not only authenticated his experience; it made the experience both understandable and accessible to others. It was also clear that the experience Jaworski described was something that any person could put to the test and act on. The proof of the pudding would be in the eating. Jaworski was dishing up a rich pudding that would take years to digest and savor.

Jaworski discovered that anyone can live a life that is remarkably meaningful. A meaningful life is not a matter of talent or I.Q. Instead, it is a matter of collaborating with one's calling and destiny. This doesn't undermine a person's free will. Instead, free will is essential if our calling is to unfold. In order for this to happen, we need to make three conscious, deliberate choices in the way we think about our lives and circumstances. First, we should never, ever assume that we are stuck. All of us are liable to deceive ourselves into thinking that we are trapped, with no way out. This is especially true in times of frustration and despair. We can get to thinking that we are imprisoned at the bottom of Dante's Inferno, without a millimeter of wiggle room, doomed to the misery of being forever chewed on by another's malice and our own shortcomings. Jaworski's first discovery involves the critical recognition that this just isn't so. We are never hopelessly stuck. We are never at a dead end or trapped in any final way. Our lives are not frozen fast or cast in cement. We are never, ever without hope. We always have options.

I will never forget a time when I suffered from a physical pain that was both new and frustrating. The clinical diagnosis was adhesive capsulitis. The common label is "frozen shoulder," and I can understand where that characterization came from. I could not move one of my arms. From the shoulder down, I was stuck. It hurt like nothing I had ever felt. I was not only in constant pain, but the pain was the only thing

I could think about. I thought I would never move my arm again—ever. A physician wasn't sure what my problem was but did shoot some cortisone into my shoulder. I don't know that the cortisone hurt, but I do know that it didn't really do any good. Fortunately, the physician had the foresight to refer me to a physical therapist who did know what was wrong. It was the physical therapist who made the diagnosis and thankfully had an effective plan for therapy. He gave me an exercise. It not only didn't hurt, but it actually gave me a millimeter or two of relief. I will never forget his saying, "This may not feel like it is doing anything, but it is actually creating some wiggle room that will allow your shoulder to free up."

When we are encapsulated in despair provoked by agonizing frustration, we can be tempted to assume that we will never enjoy an inch of meaningful movement as long as we live. This is a pitfall that Jaworski discovered we should avoid at all costs. We always have alternatives. Jaworski discovered that this reality is at the heart of the design of the whole universe. In other words, it is in the hard wiring—an inherent reality. When we recognize and embrace this first truth, we actually begin to develop wiggle room. Life begins to loosen up. The recognition that we always have options allows us to live with the freedom of genuine openness, not unlike the arrival of spring that makes it possible to open all the windows of the house so that the entire dwelling can once again breathe.

What Jaworski discovered is that options and alternatives are a metaphysical reality: to become aware of the presence of alternatives is to begin to participate in, if not become aware of, the design of the entire universe. Becoming aware of this reality requires an openness that is entirely conscious and deliberate. This openness involves a complete willingness on our part. We have to open our eyes and watch what is unfolding. This openness is a matter of autonomous choice.

The second shift in our thinking involves recognizing that the foundational order of the universe is relationships. This is true at every level—the quantum or implicate level, the macro level, and the cosmological level. Relationships are the primary substance—the stuff out of which all life is made. This is what led Fyodor Dostoevsky to observe that where two or more are gathered, there is a whole world. Relationships are the substance of life whether we are speaking about a universe consisting of two molecules or the interaction of entire galaxies. Our connections to each other are of incalculable significance. *We* are important. *We* count. Two people come to constitute a whole world when they recognize and sustain awareness of this reality.

The third and final shift in our thinking is every bit as important as the first two: each of us is essential for the unfolding of the implicate order. Essentiality lies at the core of our humanity. It is what defines us. I am essential. You are essential. We are essential. Recognizing our essentiality isn't a matter of personal conceit or a sense of superiority over others. Instead, when we come to a recognition and acceptance of our essentiality, we develop a clear understanding that we have a place in the universe that is permeated with meaning.

Joseph Jaworski discovered that when we make these three shifts in thinking, two consequences follow: First, the right people begin to come together. We meet the people we are supposed to meet. The right relationships begin to emerge—just like that. This isn't something we can force to happen. When we try to force relationships, we end up with relationships that are somehow false, inauthentic, and unproductive. When, on the other hand, we consciously embrace these shifts in our thinking, the right people begin, mysteriously, to gather. Second, when we understand that we always have options, that the fundamental constituent of the universe is relationships, and that we are essential for what is emerging and unfolding, not only do the right people begin to gather, but also the right doors open. It is our responsibility to open our eyes and to recognize the opening of the doors and to walk through them. The opening of doors is every bit as mysterious and real as the gathering of the right people.

The phenomenon that Jaworski described is called synchronicity. Carl Jung wrote about this phenomenon extensively. Here's what Jaworski said: "Arthur Koestler, paraphrasing Jung, defines 'synchronicity' as 'the seemingly accidental meeting of two unrelated causal chains in a coincidental event which appears both highly improbable and highly significant.' The people who come to you are the very people you need in relation to your commitment. Doors open, a sense of flow develops, and you find you are acting in a coherent field of people who may not even be aware of one another. You are not acting individually any longer, but out of the unfolding generative order. This is the unbroken wholeness of the implicate order out of which seemingly discrete events take place. At this point, your life becomes a series of predictable miracles."

Jaworski also discovered a connection between the mysterious synchronicity of time, place, and event, which was unfolding in his life, and the Cathedral of Chartres. The first time Jaworski visited the Cathedral, he reports being able to recognize and to sense the phenomenon of synchronicity:

This cathedral was built in the mid-thirteenth century when high gothic architecture was at its purest, and it possesses a unique symmetry and unity. Being near it and in it, I felt unity with all that was around me, a complete openness to the entire world. I intended to visit the cathedral for an hour or so, but ended up spending the entire day there, first sitting quietly and then later reflectively walking all around the vast cathedral, both inside and out. As I was there, I experienced the most unusual feeling, a sort of ringing in my ears and entire head. It's difficult for me to describe, but it was distinctly familiar. It was as if I were in a different energy field altogether. I had experienced that feeling many times out in the wilderness, but this was the first time it had happened to me in a structure built by human hands. Late that afternoon, still in the cathedral, I found myself thinking about two notions of freedom, both of which would be continually at play on this seven-week trip. The first was "freedom from," that is, freedom to get away from the oppressiveness of circumstances. . . . But another notion of freedom was beginning to make its way into my consciousness at this time, far below the surface—the freedom to follow my life's purpose with all the commitment I could muster, while at the same time, allowing life's creative forces to move through me without my control, without "making it happen." As I was to learn over time, this is by far a much more powerful way of operating. The experience at Chartres made me want to find ways to break through the limiting factors I had discovered in myself, especially fear. (Joseph Jaworski, *Synchronicity*, 38)

This is what drew me to the Cathedral. It is a complete world that is at once hospitable to the people who visit, the history of the world, and the order of the universe. Over time, I would come to know the cathedral as a place that embodies a completeness of insight and knowledge that permeates all of life. The kind of knowledge, insight, and understanding that Jaworski felt not only reverberated in and through this world; it became a source of quiet joy and a window into the delectation of mystery.

Why is this important? The Cathedral of Chartres can take us to the root of the human spirit where we drink from the fountain of the divine. Just as the builders of the Cathedral developed an entire architecture that embodies astonishing beauty, the Cathedral in turn can form the architecture of the human soul—an architecture that is alive with insight, possibility, and generativity. The artwork of the Cathedral can take us to the root of the human spirit where we encounter, know, and understand God, ourselves, and the mutual enfoldment of the two. It embodies the primordial substance with which we can build our lives in communion with God and one another. It is just that important.

THE CATHEDRAL, THE
WORLD, AND EXPERIENCE

> *Rosch said that primary knowing arises "by means of interconnected wholes (rather than isolated contingent parts) and by means of timeless, direct presentation (rather than through stored representations)."*
>
> **—Joseph Jaworski,** *Source*

There is an image from the late Middle Ages that comes from both St. Thomas and Dante, who get their image from Leviticus. Animals that are cloven footed and chew the cud are clean and therefore fit for human consumption. St. Thomas and Dante used this image as a metaphor for leadership: They used "cloven footed" as a metaphor for discerning the difference between good and evil, and "chewing the cud" as a metaphor for reflection. We use the phrase "chewing on a good idea," or digesting it. It makes reflection real.

I have been chewing on Jaworski's experience with the Cathedral of Chartres for over a decade. I have digested his experience both in the Cathedral and in my subsequent reflections, and I have done so because I wanted, as much as possible, to embrace and to understand his experience. As I sorted my thoughts, two emerged as essential. The first had to do with the nature of his experience. What is it about being in this Cathedral that is so compelling? The second had to do with assimilating this experience into the whole of life. When engaged in the Cathedral, there is a certain level of palpable intensity. If not impossible, it is difficult at best to sustain this level of experience. I was wondering what to make of this.

What is it about fully experiencing the Cathedral of Chartres that is so compelling? What can we observe? I think it essential to begin with the observation that the Cathedral of Chartres is a whole world: It is complete. Everything is related to everything else. The meaning of the Cathedral resides in the interconnections. If I am studying a window or a sculpture, I am mindful that the work of art that I am studying is connected to all other art within a gothic architecture of interconnected wholeness. I also come to observe that the interconnections are not only complete, but they also are generative: they fill the fully engaged, thoughtful imagination with the same creativity and insight that went into their design and composition. Being fully present and engaged with the Cathedral is thrilling because it fills the imagination with all of the insight and generativity that a human imagination can take in. The contents of the artwork and architecture bring the imagination into communion with the order of the world. This is, if I may say so, heady stuff. It is astonishing. It is compelling. It is completely mesmerizing—provided I am willing to stay with it.

It is mesmerizing because we who visit the Cathedral are not complete or whole. We are human. Being human, we are incomplete, unfinished, and still emerging. The Cathedral of Chartres is complete, finished, and whole. What happens in the Cathedral is something like this. We enter a created place of architectural, artistic, and metaphysical contact between two worlds—the world that the

Cathedral embodies and our own embodied selves. We who are still emerging meet and encounter the generativity of the Cathedral. We who are incomplete meet the complete. We who are temporal meet the eternal. We who are inconclusive meet the concluded. We who are unfinished and inadequate meet the finished and the completely adequate. We who are as yet unrealized meet the fully realized. We whose knowledge is still developing meet the knowledge of an artistic memory that is fully developed in its generativity. We who are particular and individual meet the universal and the comprehensive. We who are malleable meet the rock solid. We who are finite meet the infinite. The Cathedral is compelling because we meet something of a completely different kind. The marvel is that we find that our own lives and the world that the Cathedral embodies are mysteriously fit for each other. The generativity of the interconnections of the Cathedral directly addresses our humanity and fills our imaginations with insight, new possibilities, and acres of hope. This is an intensely compelling experience.

It is not, however, an intensity of experience that is easy to sustain. It took me quite a bit of time to understand the reason for the fading of the intensity. I am responsible for taking the experience of marvel and the numinous and making it my own. I am responsible for taking my own experience and my responsibility for others to the life-giving interconnections that the Cathedral embodies. This is an act of both imagination and will. I found that in prayer (interaction with God) and in meditation (awareness of the emerging generative order of the universe) I had both the opportunity and responsibility to take circumstances for which I am responsible into the heart of the Source of generativity and life. The Cathedral is one of the most complete embodiments of the Source that I have encountered. It was calling on me to make it my own.

Making it my own would involve everything—my reading, my reflection, and my interaction with others. Everything counts; nothing is excluded. I would have to become open to being my best self and to knowing others at their best. It would turn out that knowing one another at our best would be well worth the effort, for this would involve what is best in my own humanity.

KNOWING EACH OTHER AT OUR BEST

Such knowing is "open" rather than determinate; and a sense of unconditional value, rather than conditional usefulness, is an inherent part of the act of knowing itself. Action from awareness is claimed to be spontaneous, rather than the result of decision making; it is compassionate since it is based on wholes larger than the self; and it can be shockingly effective.
—**Eleanor Rosch,** quoted in Joseph Jaworski, *Source*

I t was a Monday morning. It happened to be the Monday after Easter. It was also my second Monday on a new job. On the previous Monday, I had conducted an initial team meeting. It was introductory. I was the new leader. We were all meeting each other for the first time. The team was anxious. And by the time I arrived, we were all pretending *not* to be anxious! On the one hand, they genuinely wanted a new leader; on the other, we knew very little about each other. There was lots of risk. Uncertainty filled the air like an eastern North Carolina fog.

One week later, it was time for my first *regular* staff meeting with a new team. In order to become a team, I thought it important to engage the team in dialogue. I think of dialogue as important for many reasons. One of those reasons involves a combination of a belief and hope: I hope and believe that the destiny and work of our team will unfold as we *all* bring ideas to the table. From the get-go, I wanted our team to grow to understand that each member of the team counts. I use the word "member" instead of "part." I wanted the people on our team to begin to think of themselves as "members" of a team, as opposed to, say, "parts" of a team. In my way of thinking, "parts" are akin to machinery. People aren't machines. We are born with imagination and the capacity for creativity. Treating people as parts of a machine dehumanizes us and undermines the team. I much prefer, with the poet Alan Tate, to think of people not as parts, but as members, because member is akin to human dignity and interaction. To say that someone is a *member* of a team is to recognize the humanity of each person.

One of the most important "lessons" I have learned over the years is that people are people, not objects. I am at my best when I see the humanity in each person, and I am at my worst when I refuse or fail to do so. It is essential that I treat people as people—both in my direct interactions with them and behind their backs. It is all too easy to fall into the habit of characterizing someone in ways that degrade his or her humanity and then acting as though my characterization were the truth. What I had to learn (and this was my responsibility and mine alone) was that when I degrade someone else—even in my ways of thinking about the person—I degrade myself. On the other hand, when I see a person as a person, I position myself to respond to the person's humanity and at the same time strengthen my own. I have also learned that when I actively seek to know people at their best, I complement and support their efforts to be their best as well. This doesn't guarantee that others will be their best, but it creates a climate in which we can flourish together.

This kind of thinking also plays into leadership. I am not at my best as a top-down kind of leader. I do better when *we* do better, and *we* do better when everyone brings something to the table. I try to create a climate of hospitality and respect in which meaning can unfold within the dialogue of the team. The team itself might create or discover meaning. Meaning unfolds in the dialogue of the group, and at some critical point, the team itself gives birth to that meaning. There are a whole bunch of reasons this is important to me, not the least of which is that I recognize that I don't have all the answers. Worse, there are times when I have *no* answers. And even when I do have *some* answers, others often have answers that are better than answers I bring to the table. My daughter Jaime has a phrase: "That's the coolest thing ever!" I think it's the coolest thing ever when each member of the team begins to understand, "I count, and so does every other person at the table." When we truly regard each other with respect, and when we truly open our hearts to the treasures that dwell in the hearts and minds of colleagues—other members of the team—meanings and ways of doing things unfold among us that are both new and astonishing.

So it's our first staff meeting. I wanted to do my part to begin to transform us into a team, and I thought the story of Abraham a great place to begin. There are many reasons for choosing Abraham, not the least of which is that Abraham was a great listener, and listening isn't a bad thing if you're trying to build a team. If we are going to become an *effective* team, listening is *essential*. I have to care about what others have to say. I have to drink in their words, without interruption and without condescension. If I am going to become a good listener, I have to treasure the person speaking and to treasure that person's words. Abraham had that gift.

We began in Genesis 12 because that's where Abram's story begins (it isn't till Genesis 17 that his name is lengthened to Abraham). The words are straightforward. Abram heard a voice. It was the voice of God. God gave Abram simple, clear, direct instructions: "Go from your country and your kindred and your father's house to the land that I will show you. And I will make you a great nation, and I will bless you and make your name great, so that you will be a blessing. I will bless those who bless you, and him who dishonors you I will curse, and in you all the families of the earth shall be a blessing" (12:1–3). Abram did exactly as he was told.

It was after we had spent a half hour in conversation that a member of the team asked a question: "How was Abraham able to recognize the voice?" For me, this is a wonderful question for several reasons, not the least of which is that I am not only interested in recognizing and hearing the voice of God, but I cannot think of anything more important. I realize that there are people in this world who regard the possibility of hearing God a bona fide impossibility. Some who think this way are militant atheists. They believe that because there is no God, there is no voice of God to recognize. I also realize that there are people who believe that God exists but that it is somewhere between unlikely and impossible that we can hear the voice of God. And I realize that there are people who *claim* to hear the voice of God but are in fact suffering from delusions that stem from an inflated sense of their own importance. Reasons to object to the idea that we can hear God's voice are no doubt more complex and nuanced than I have represented. My purpose isn't so much to be exhaustive in representing objections, but to acknowledge that objections are real.

For me, it doesn't make sense to make an a priori assumption that God doesn't exist, nor does it make sense to believe that if God exists, the possibility of recognizing God's voice is at best remote. I think it makes more sense to take a story like Abram's and to explore his life with all of the respect, openness and understanding that I can muster. I also think it right that we extend this same measure of respect and understanding to the person (or persons) who wrote Abram's story. If, in reading Abram's story, there are insights to be gleaned, those insights will come only if I seek to understand Abram at his best. In other words, Abram's story will open up the treasure chest of its insight to the degree that I am willing to know both Abram and his story at their best. I don't think this a matter of naïve innocence or gullibility on my part. I have learned that I can know people and have strong relationships with them if I am willing to know them at their best, including the best that they aspire to be. This doesn't mean that I am so dumb as to think that people are always their best selves and never up to no good. I believe that all of us can be our best selves, and I also believe that all of us can be up to no good at least some of the time. I also realize that some of us can be up to no good more than others. I don't believe that any of us are totally honest; I do believe that all of us find it difficult to be honest with ourselves. All of us have blind spots. But with that, I believe that all of us can work at being honest with both ourselves and others. It is more likely that people will be their best selves if I will seek to know them at their best. I believe that most of us want to be our best and that all of us find being our best to be a struggle more times than we care to admit. At the same time, we will all have an easier time being our best selves in a climate where people seek to see us as people, not as objects, labels, or categories, and to know us at our best.

This is the reason that I want to approach Abram and his story with respect and sympathy. I want to know Abram at his best, and I want to know what the story is trying to convey—both the intent of the writers and the effect that the story has. The story itself will show us Abram at his worst, with all of his flaws. There are occasions in the story when Abram's behavior is shocking, if not horrifying. We will also see that Abram, like many of us, found learning from his sins and mistakes to be agonizingly difficult. But if we stick with Abram, we will discover that Abram's sins and mistakes did not finally undermine what was actually unfolding in the totality of Abram's life—a facility for knowing both God and the mystery of the unfolding of God's power in the world.

This brings us back to that initial question: How was Abram able to recognize God's voice? I was delighted that a colleague on our team would ask it because the answer will provide a small opening through which we, too, can recognize God's voice, God's presence, and something of God's creativity and generativity as they emerge and unfold in our world—not only right before our eyes but sometimes because of actions we are willing to take to bring God's generativity to fruition.

RECOGNIZING
THE VOICE

Speaking, therefore, seems to be created out of an active silence. In quantum physics there is also a kind of vibrant silence; it is called the vacuum state, the state of total and absolute emptiness. The theories of modern physics indicate that this state of nothingness is in fact an infinite ocean of energy in potential. All the energy within our universe—the energy of suns and galaxies—is as a mere flicker on this vast ocean of nothingness.

—F. David Peat, *Blackfoot Physics*

Then Arthur began to outline the process for tapping into this source—what he called "knowing." He said, "This inner knowing comes from here," pointing to his heart. "In a sense, there is no decision making," he said. "What you do just becomes obvious. A totally different set of rules applies. You hang back. You're more like a surfer or a really good racecar driver. You don't act out of deduction, you act out of an inner feeling; you're not even thinking."

—Joseph Jaworski, *Source*

"How was Abram able to recognize the voice? How did he know it was God?"

In response to the question, I shared how I was thinking about this very question on the previous day. It was early on the morning on Easter Sunday, 2012. I was sitting in a hotel room drinking coffee, pondering the story of Abram, wondering just how it was that he was able to recognize the voice of God. An insight visited my imagination in the form of an intuition that was both modest and simple. Abram was familiar with silence. He knew what genuine quiet sounded like. Silence was a part of his world—so much so that it would have caused Abram no discomfort. For him, quietness wasn't the exception; it was the norm. We rarely experience the kind of quiet that Abram knew. Sitting in that hotel room in the wee hours of the morning, it was easy to open the door to this insight. It was "quiet"—at least by our standards. But in response to my intuition, I listened to the "quiet." There was much to hear. I could hear the buzz of the air conditioner. I could hear the hum of the refrigerator. I could hear doors opening and closing in the hallway outside my room. I could hear people walking on the floor in the room above. The sounds I could easily hear fit our twenty-first century definition of quiet, but for Abram, it would have been noisy. Abram's quiet was the real thing. When the voice spoke to Abram—whether in the intuition of his imagination or actually producing sound waves that knocked on his ear drum, the voice would have been easier for Abram to recognize. For Abram, the voice of God did not compete with a cacophony of mind-numbing noise. Abram lived and moved in an aural climate in which the voice could be recognized with alacrity.

For me, the implications are clear: it is good to develop comfort with being silent and enjoying quietness. It is good that a sense of quiet become familiar. I am not suggesting that it is necessary to go cold turkey on chatter, music, talk radio, or the internet. Nor do I think it insulting to point out that we live in a stimuli-saturated world. What I do think is that by creating openings of silence and by entering those openings for longer periods of time, we can become more comfortable with a quality of quiet that will allow us to recognize and to hear what is most genuine. This creates an internal climate in which we can enjoy stillness. A deep sense of stillness allows for the first inklings of quiet curiosity to emerge.

CURIOSITY

Arthur described the process to us in unmistakable terms, explaining that it entails three major stages or "elements." The first thing you do, he said, is "observe, observe, observe." This kind of intense observation "might take days, or hours, or fractions of a second as in martial arts or sports"; then you "reflect and retreat— allow the inner knowing to emerge." Finally, he said, you "act swiftly, with a natural flow."

—Joseph Jaworski, *Source*

I t was a small beginning—like the sowing of a single seed. The seed germinated and began to take root. The tree would be a long time in its growth. A root structure developed beneath the surface. The roots would both anchor the tree and drink in both water and nutrients. Eventually, something would unfold enough that it emerged from the earth. The tree began to drink in light, which initiated additional development and growth. The sunshine was glorious, but the rains and wind were at times fierce. I remember reading about the biosphere just north of Tucson. It was an experiment in a living space that was completely enclosed. My wife Nancy and I visited the biosphere when we were living in Tucson. I remember reading that the biggest challenge to the biosphere was the trees. They were wimpy—completely lacking in vitality, heft, and health. The reason was simple: there was no wind in the biosphere. To become healthy, trees need wind. The wind provides what in the gym we call strength training—the resistance that is necessary for development, growth, and vitality. If you want to see a person completely wanting of vitality, look for the person who tries to live in absolute comfort, insulated from problems and difficulties to challenge ingenuity, creativity, and effort. To develop fully, trees need the wind. So did my curiosity.

Curiosity is the seed that was sown early in my life. I became aware that curiosity in part defines us as humans. I began to understand curiosity when I was in my twenties. I was in seminary. We were studying the thirteenth chapter of Matthew, which includes not only seed parables, but also Jesus's Parable of the Treasure Hidden in the Field. In this parable, Jesus likens the kingdom of heaven to a treasure, hidden in a field, which a man found, covered back up, and in his joy went and sold everything that he had and purchased the field. What intrigued me about this parable was what the parable conceals—*doesn't* tell us. We don't know anything about the owner of the field—his identity, his life, his dreams, or who he is; nor does the parable give any direct description about the owner's relationship to the treasure. Jesus doesn't tell us if the owner knows about the treasure. But upon reflection, it certainly seems unlikely that the owner would have sold the field had he known about the treasure that his field contained. I also began to realize that we don't know anything about the man who *found* the treasure. We know nothing of his identity, nor do we know how he found the treasure. Was he looking for it? Was he trespassing? Did he know where to look? Did he have intelligence? Had he overheard someone else talking about the treasure? And if he didn't know where to look, by the time he actually found the treasure, did he leave the field looking as though a large gopher had torn up the place? And then there's the value of the treasure, which Jesus also says nothing about. How much was the treasure worth? How much was the man worth? How much risk was involved in his liquidating his assets?

We can't know this for certain, but it seems to me not only that the owner of the field didn't know about the presence of the treasure, but also that he ultimately got snookered. The man who purchased the field obviously knew that the treasure was there. That was why he went to all the trouble to purchase the field. It is also clear that the man was far more interested in the treasure than in the real estate

Here's what I find most fascinating about this parable: it provokes curiosity; it causes us to ask questions. It creates a sense of mystery that causes us to wonder. That is one of the parable's effects. As I began to study the Bible in earnest, it began to dawn on me that the passages I was reading not only had a message, but they also had an effect: stories don't just say something; they also *do* something. They create effects in our imaginations. Some stories provoke anger or frustration. Some create joy. Some stories create moods that can be pensive, reflective, dark, vibrant, mysterious, somber, or tender. Stories do that. They carry messages, but they also affect us— sometimes deeply. Good stories are like that. They do something to us. They engage us, and they work their wonders. The Parable of the Treasure Hidden in the Field is that kind of story. It has an effect, and the effect is to create a sense of wonder by provoking and enlivening our curiosity. The parable engages our imaginations and heightens our awareness. It positions us for insight and discovery. The parable draws us into Mystery by presenting us with a mystery to be pondered. If we are willing to engage the parable, the parable engages us in an active discovery of things that matter greatly.

It would take me years to learn that curiosity is a great gift. It lies at the heart of our humanity. To be effective, to lead us to truth, curiosity also requires a measure of resistance. It isn't good to allow curiosity to take us everywhere it wants to go. Some pathways are better left untrodden and unexplored.

Jesus understood that if we are willing to allow our curiosities to be fully engaged, and if we are willing to commit our curiosities to understanding, our curiosities will ultimately lead us to the treasure hidden in the field of our imaginations and lives.

The treasure is teeming with great mystery.

FROM CURIOSITY TO MYSTERY

Mystery today means something impenetrable to the mind, something never to be understood. To St. Paul and to the early Christian thinkers it was on the contrary the particular object of intelligence, its fullest nourishment. The musterion is something so rich in intelligible content, so inexhaustibly full of delectation for the mind, that no contemplation can ever reach its end. It is an eternal delectation of the mind.
—**Claude Tresmontant,** *A Study of Hebrew Thought*

I can pinpoint the moment in my life when in dawned on me that Mystery is the thing. I was in Chartres. I had taken a slim volume by Claude Tresmontant. Why this particular writer? He was a favorite of Flannery O'Connor, and Flannery O'Connor is a favorite of mine. What I like best about O'Connor is that her novels and short stories pick up where science and rational explanation end. As a writer of fiction who was a woman of thoughtful faith, Flannery O'Connor was always interested in the things that science cannot explain, and the things that science cannot explain involve mystery:

> If the writer believes that our life is and will remain essentially mysterious, if he looks upon us as beings existing in a created order to whose laws we freely respond, then what he sees on the surface will be of interest to him only as he can go through it into an experience of mystery itself. His kind of fiction will always be pushing its own limits outward toward the limits of mystery, because for this kind of writer, the meaning of a story does not begin except at a depth where adequate motivation and adequate psychology and the various determinations have been exhausted. Such a writer will be interested in what we don't understand rather than in what we do (Flannery O'Connor, "The Grotesque in Southern Fiction").

As I began to explore O'Connor's ways of knowing more deeply, I discovered that she was particularly fond of Tresmontant, a French biblical scholar and metaphysician. So when I visited the Cathedral in Chartres, I took a copy of his book on Hebrew thought. I was stunned. I still am.

There are two things that Claude Tresmontant is interested in: metaphysics and mystery. The word *metaphysics* can at first seem to be intimidating, but it's not a difficult concept. The prefix, *meta*, means above, after, or beyond. In that sense, the word means *after physics*, or *beyond physics*. The word *metaphysics* refers to the way the world—both material and immaterial—is formatted, or put together. To involve oneself in metaphysics is to engage in the search to understand connections. They can be connections within the world. They can be connections between people and the world. Metaphysics can involve connections between what we read in literature and how we live, art and physics, justice and real-life circumstances, generativity and a problem that stares us in the face. Metaphysics can also involve connections within art and literature, and then, those connections to the world, or to science, or to decision-making. To engage in the discovery of the meaning of life is to engage in metaphysics. To explore the nature of creativity is to engage in metaphysics as well. Physicist David Bohm would talk about the "unbroken wholeness" between thinking, intent, and the material world. This is a matter of metaphysics.

From his study of the Old and New Testaments, Tresmontant came to an insight: the Hebrews held certain metaphysical assumptions, ways of thinking about God and the world of materiality. They saw God, meaning, truth, and mystery as completely embodied in the material world. The Hebrews didn't conceptualize God as some sort of gaseous, disembodied spirit. They saw the workings, the involvement of God, as completely embodied in material reality. The faith and understanding of the Hebrews was as rock solid as Mount Sinai and the stone tables. There was nothing disembodied or ethereal about Hebrew thought.

That thought—that kind of metaphysical thinking—is what enabled the Hebrews to know and understand God. Had their thinking been dualistic, had they thought of the world of spirit as something completely separate from the material world, they could not have known and understood God or his world with the depth and profundity that they did. What the Hebrews discovered is that Mystery is completely embodied in the world and is present for us to discover, understand, and participate in.

When Tresmontant looked at the metaphysics that the Bible embodies, he recognized that connections are everything. Truth is connected to creativity, to freedom, to dialogue, to action, to consciousness, to conscience, to the human heart, and to mystery. Tresmontant recognized that we are responsible for our own thoughts because we create them. He recognized that what the Bible calls the human heart is the center of our humanity, where we make our most important choices. If we choose, if we commit to truth, then truth opens a dialogue—both within an individual human heart and between people who are mutually committed to truth. When we commit to truth, we discover that our actions can collaborate both with divine will and with the order of the universe. We become aware that the way in which we seek to understand the world involves spiritual intelligence. We learn to recognize and to understand not only the germinating of the seed, but also the entire growth of the plant or tree from germination to the production of fruit and flowering. We then learn to see the connections between our understanding of the totality of the conception and development of the plant with the totality of our conception and development as human beings. The seat of this understanding involves human consciousness, which in turn embodies human conscience. We also recognize the connection between human conscience and the thinking of God. The ways in which we think about and measure the world are linked to ways in which God is involved in the world. We develop our capacities for recognizing the presence of God as we develop our facility for creativity, dialogue, and communion with God, the world, and fellow humans. We come to a mutual understanding of the essentiality of both relationships and each person with whom we are related. Perhaps most important, we grow in our understanding that mystery is not only ultimate reality, but it is also something that we are created to explore and to understand. The words of Claude Tresmontant, from *Hebrew Thought*, are frequently close at hand:

> Mystery today means something impenetrable to the mind, something never to be understood. To St. Paul and to the early Christian thinkers it was on the contrary the particular object of intelligence, its fullest nourishment. The *musterion* is something so rich in intelligible content, so inexhaustibly full of delectation for the mind, that no contemplation can ever reach its end. It is an eternal delectation of the mind.

Mystery, in other words, is not something that is inaccessible. It is an ever present, inexhaustible, compelling reality that we can relish and explore. As I write these words, I am working in Gladstone's Library in Wales. The Library is a wonder for those of us who love reading and writing. It's a residential theological library. Everything is included, including wonderful meals. They are, to use Tresmontant's word, delectable. This isn't fast food, and the meals aren't the kind of thing you scarf. You don't eat on the run. You savor both the delectable cuisine and the conversation, for most people come to the Library to do their own work. We work separately on whatever projects we bring with us. The man at the library table next to me, with whom I have shared several meals, is taking a few days for reading. A woman, several tables away, is writing her doctoral dissertation. We work in silence, and the silence is a welcome climate to our tasks. But during meals, we talk about our work, and the delectation of the meal is matched by the delectation of ideas and the sense of wonder that develops as we discover the connections between our ideas and our work.

That's the kind of thing that Claude Tresmontant discovered about the Hebrews: they had devoted their life together to the delectation of mystery. It wasn't an individual matter. They were in communion with one another, and God was at the heart of their communion. They understood, through their experience—their interaction with God and with one another—that Mystery is embodied in their communion with one another and the world. Mystery was the reason for their life together. This was the assumption with which they approached each other, God, and God's world. Because of that assumption, and within that assumption, knowledge of God—an experience of knowing that was direct and primary—began to unfold. It was there for their exploration. It was there for all to behold and to treasure.

THE EXPANSE

There exists an eternally creative Source of infinite potential that lies beyond the orders of time. It exists before the sequential orders of time and is found beneath the levels of increasing subtlety from which the orders of mind and matter emerge. It is the one underlying Source constantly giving birth to the universe at every eternal moment. It is the wellspring of the universe itself.

—Joseph Jaworski, *Source*

It is a small sculpture that portrays the second day of creation, from Genesis 1. The sculpture is on the middle arch of the north portal in the Cathedral of Chartres. The north portal portrays stories from the Old Testament, just as the south portal portrays stories from the New. The sculpture caught my attention because I had been giving thought to the seven day story in Genesis 1. I was particularly mesmerized by the second day, for on this day, God creates an expanse right in the middle of the abyss—the vast unfathomable chaos of waters. God calls the expanse the heavens. But for the Genesis story, it's important to recognize that the second day involves the creation of an expanse—right in the midst of chaos. What struck me about the sculpture in the north portal is that it portrays the expanse in all of its simplicity.

The sculpture itself is not a beauty when compared to Michelangelo's *Pietá* or Donotello's *Mary Magdelene*. This sculpture is a simple, three-part structure. It has a top, a bottom, and a middle section. The top and bottom depict the waters of chaos, which are layered and wavy. The waters of chaos are separated by a large space, which represents the heavens that are in the middle. The sculpture conveys the idea that God created the heavens in the midst of the deep—the waters of chaos. The deep is an ominous, threatening abyss. The heavens are open and spacious.

The creation story in Genesis 1 begins in darkness and chaos. In the beginning, the substance of creation was formless and beyond measure. It was also lifeless. Then two things happened. First, the breath of God was blowing over the waters. Then God said, "Let there be light." God saw that light was good and separated the light from the darkness. God called the light day and the darkness night. This creative action also initiated time, for there was evening and then morning: the first day.

It is on the second day that form begins to emerge. This is the idea that is so perfectly sculpted in the north portal of the Cathedral. God initiates the creation of space by creating an expanse in the midst of the abyss. The expanse separates the waters, dividing them on two sides of the expanse. The creation of the expanse forms the basis of everything that God accomplishes in creation. On the third day of creation, an expanse of earth emerges so that land is now separated from the waters, just as the waters were separated from the waters on the second day. God then plants seed on the land, which when watered initiates the germination of the seed, which develops expanses of plant life emerging and unfolding from the seed which is rooted in the earth. On the fourth day, our attention is redirected to the expanse of the heavens, where God creates the sun, moon, and stars, each of which is portrayed as an expanse within the expanse of the heavens. The expanse within the expanse is what facilitates sight, seasons, years, and understanding. Because of the light—expanses within the expanse—the conditions are in place for all creatures to see and for humans to develop knowledge and understanding.

On the fifth day, life expands in the seas and in the expanse of the heavens, for God creates fish and birds, male and female, which God commands to be fruitful and multiply and perpetuate life. On the sixth day, the creation of life moves towards greater sophistication and complexity, first with animal life, and finally with human life— male and female—as the pinnacle of creation. Humans are created in the image of God. Much is conveyed in this insight: humans have a dignity that comes directly from the sovereignty of God. It is a dignity that can be felt and known through intuition. Human dignity cannot be isolated and measured in a laboratory. Human dignity is, however, a matter of the mystery that can be known in our common experience beyond doubt. What is required for this mystery to be known includes a fair measure of human willingness coupled with humility.

One of the matters that characterize human dignity involves our capacity for imagination. Humans are created in the image of God. *Image* lies at the heart of *imagination*. Imagination is something that we share with God. And if we look at the image of God that Genesis 1 portrays, we become witnesses to God's creativity. God imagines ends that do not yet exist. The ends involve order, time, space, life, cooperation, germination, metabolism, light, breath, the willingness to see, and creativity. Because our imaginations involve the capacity to conceptualize space, we have the capacity to recognize not only the expanse that unfolds on the second day of creation; we also have the capacity to see the connection between the expanse that God created on the second day with other expanses of similar significance. As we shall see, Abram not only had the capacity to recognize expanses within the expanse, but his willingness to exercise his powers of recognition led to his understanding both his relationship to God and his place in God's world. Abram formed his understanding into an altar.

THE GENESIS ALTAR

Metaphysics formats and enables experience and, in turn, molds scientific, social, and individual reality. It provides a description of human experience that satisfies a deep longing within us.

—Joseph Jaworski, *Source*

The first thing that Abram did after arriving in Canaan was to build an altar. He had made a long journey from Haran to Canaan. His travels brought him to Shechem, to the Oak of Moreh. As soon as he arrived, he built an altar. Abram then travelled to the hill country east of Bethel. There, he built a second altar.

The building of altars is intriguing. The writer doesn't give us reasons for the altars. There are no sacrifices mentioned, as there are in Genesis 15 and 22, where sacrifices are central to the story. God does not direct Abram to build the altars, nor does God give any instructions concerning what Abram is to do with the altars. Abram simply builds two altars. That is all that the writer tells us. The writer describes the action plainly, leaving it to us to observe. It is through observation that we discover what Abram is up to.

The story is straightforward. Abram's father, Terah, had taken the family and left Ur with the intent to travel to Canaan. When they had gotten half way, they settled in Haran, where Terah's family remained for the rest of his life. Terah died at the age of 205.

After Terah's death, Abram heard a voice. God did not *appear* to Abram (that comes later). Instead, God spoke, calling on Abram to leave the place of his father's house and to go to a place that God would show Abram. In other words, the voice said, "Follow me." The voice promised to make Abram's name great and to transform his people into a great nation. Abram would be a blessing, and in him families would be blessed.

The story doesn't tell us whether Abram heard the voice audibly or as the still small voice of intuition. Either way, the voice that Abram recognized and heard resonated with his consciousness and filled his imagination. Abram found the voice compelling, for he trusted it completely. Abram responded in full measure. He packed up everything (and everyone) and followed.

Abram gave his consent freely. He was under no compulsion. God did not threaten Abram. God didn't tell Abram that if he refused to follow, there would be hell to pay. There was no coercion. There was, however, clarity and respect. The voice addressed Abram directly, simply, and plainly.

The issue of consent is important because there was great risk on Abram's part. On the one hand, the voice was making a promise of incalculable import: the benefit offered was enormous—not only for Abram, but also for his descendants. The voice was promising that both Abram and his family would inherit and embody the blessing—the life-giving breath—of God. This is not the kind of promise it would have been wise for Abram to ignore. But the risk to Abram was great not only for the sheer investment of time, energy, and effort, but also because at this point in the story, Abram and God had no history together. Abram stood at the very beginning—the genesis—of his involvement with God. The book of Genesis does not describe any prior relationship between God and Abram. As far as their relationship is concerned, they were at square one. For Abram, and for the people who depended on Abram, the risk was huge. No one in Abram's family had been where Abram is going. God offered Abram no road map; nor did God tell Abram where they are going. Abram had only the voice, which was saying, "Follow me."

The risk would involve effort on everybody's part, and the effort would be considerable. My wife Nancy and I recently moved from Kansas to North Carolina. Moving isn't easy. The effort taxes everyone, and this, in spite of the fact that we had wonderful help, including an excellent, professional moving company. Even with the help we received, and our travelling by car and by plane, we were still tired from the ordeal! The effort required of Abram and his family would have been staggering. This was no small commitment. God was calling on Abram to move everyone and everything—the entire family and all their possessions. Abram gave his consent. He also devoted all of his effort and energies to responding. His response was decisive and complete. The story reports no arguing, no reluctance, and no reservations.

In calling (as opposed to seducing or coercing) Abram, God addresses Abram as a person who is free. This creates the conditions in which Abram can in turn respond to God freely. Abram does so by engaging the voice. The voice of God has addressed both Abram's imagination and his capacity for free choice.

By addressing Abram's un-coerced imagination with a promise, God allowed Abram to give his consent freely and to engage in taking the risk. Risk taking lay at the heart of Abram's entrusting himself to God. We the reader are at liberty to observe that the risk was not reckless; but it was risk all the same, especially in view of the fact that Abram was at the beginning of a relationship with God. Abram's relationship with God did not yet involve the comfort of familiarity; that would require time.

It was not until they arrived at their destination that God would, for the first time, *appear* to Abram. It is as if God's appearing was in response to Abram's proven willingness to entrust himself to the voice. God appeared to Abram when he arrived at Shechem, at the oak of Moreh. It was immediately after God appeared that Abram built an altar. God did not direct Abram to do so. Abram built the altar from the freedom of his own imagination: it was *his* idea. This, if I may say so, was a curious thing to do. Why would Abram build an altar—at this time and place, and at this point in the story? And just as important, how do we go about finding the answer that conveys the greatest insight?

I'd like to suggest that we begin with what is unfolding in Abram's imagination and link that to the circumstances in which Abram finds himself. I'd like to suggest that we compare what we can reasonably surmise about what is going on in Abram's imagination with the act of building the altar. What can we observe?

We can first observe that Abram implemented God's instructions completely. Abram was taken up with what God was telling him. I think it reasonable to observe that as one day of listening to this compelling voice was followed by another day of listening to this compelling voice, Abram not only grew familiar with the voice, but also the relationship between Abram and the voice developed, grew, was strengthened, and became, ultimately, fulfilling. Finally, the voice appeared; it became visible. Abram was now able to see what he had been hearing.

It was at this point that Abram built an altar. What is the altar? It is a platform of assembled rock on which Abram would have enkindled a fire. We can observe its significance by comparing it to what has been happening in Abram's interaction with God. Just as the voice of God, who has finally appeared to Abram, has been leading Abram on a journey across the land to this place, so does Abram build an altar on which he enkindles a fire that Abram can see. The altar reproduces and preserves a memory of God's involvement with Abram. Now that Abram has an idea of God's appearance to connect to God's voice, he can safeguard the experience and memory of his travels in God's presence as a source of communion. In other words, the altar is like the land on which Abram has travelled, and the fire is the embodiment of God, who first inflamed his imagination and finally appeared to Abram.

The best descriptor I can offer for Abram's altar is metaphysical space—a physical place that embodies a connection between Abram's imagination and his involvement with God. Abram responds to his involvement with God by designating a place on the earth that Abram associates with God, including God's speaking to him, leading him, and appearing to him. It seems reasonable to assume that Abram enkindled fire on the altar. In stories that follow, there are fires in both Genesis 15 and 22. The story also seems to intimate that God's appearance at least resembles fire, if God does not appear precisely *as* fire or *in* fire. I think this a reasonable assumption in view of what unfolds in the book of Exodus where God appears to Moses in the burning bush in Exodus 3 and descends in fire in Exodus 19.

The altar is a space on the earth designated to embody Abram's interaction with the mystery of God. The altar provides a solid physical means by which Abram can keep his imagination connected to his primary experience with God. In that sense, the building of the altar involves the creation of a simple, completely accessible monument that embodies Abram's engagement with God. Abram's building of the altar is akin to the artist who builds a living monument of an experience of self-evident profundity. By the time Abram builds his altar, his experience of God has reached a high level of development. It has moved beyond the first intimations of an intuition. Abram has recognized the voice of God in his imagination. He has pondered the voice, reflected on the voice, and acted on it. The voice had Abram's full and complete attention. When the voice finally appeared, his response was to build an altar—the physical expression and embodiment of his inner awareness of the voice and his outer engagement with the voice that has led Abram as he has as acted on and implemented the calling and directions of the voice with which Abram at first resonated. This is the sense in which the altar is metaphysical space: it is the outward physical embodiment of Abram's interactive experience with God who both spoke to Abram and led him—all of which were completely self-evident. These first altars provide the metaphysical means of remembrance: they allow Abram to re-enkindle fresh connections to his primary experience with God.

By building the altar, Abram also establishes a connection to the world of creation. We can participate in this connection.

The Altar, the Expanse, and the Image of God

Meaning is not final. We are continuously discovering it. And that discovery of meaning is itself a part of the reality. This worldview assumes a universal coherence and an all-encompassing principle that runs throughout the system at all levels. "We inhabit a universe that is alive with meaning and is conscious at all levels," Bohm told me.

—Joseph Jaworski, *Source*

A t the heart of the genius of Genesis are connections that the story allows us to see.

When we read Genesis we see, with the eye of imagination, created space. When we recognize created space, we can then see the connections between created spaces. Just as the creation of space is an act of imagination, so is our ability to recognize the connections between created spaces.

At the core of our humanity lies our capacity for imagination. It is what defines us. Imagination is also directly linked to free will, our human capacity to give and withhold consent. Genesis portrays a relationship in which imagination and free choice operate hand-in-glove. Genesis also portrays an un-severed relationship between imagination and the image of God. On the sixth day, humans are created in the image of God. *Image* is at the heart of imagination (*imag*ination). If we read Genesis 1 with an eye to answering the question, what is the image of God that the story portrays, what we observe is that God is creating, and God does so by means of imagination: God imagines ends that do not yet exist, and God then speaks, utilizing the primordial substance of the formless void to create a world. The world that results is a creation that comes from the imagination of God. One essential matter that Genesis 1 implies in observing that God creates us in his image is that *we have the capacity for creativity at the heart of which is human imagination.* Sans imagination, humanity is compromised.

Both the image of God and human imagination necessitate a high degree of freedom, which is necessary for both the fullness of imagination and human creativity. Without respect for the capacity to give consent, there is no true freedom.

God did not coerce Abram, nor did God seduce him. God called Abram, and in doing so, honored Abram's free will. Abram was not free to say yes if he was not also free to say no. For God to address Abram's imagination with a compelling, but un-coerced call was for God to express the greatest of respect for Abram's having been created in God's image—with imagination, the ability to envision ends that do not yet exist, and the capacity to give and withhold consent.

The writer of Genesis makes it possible for the reader to make the connection between Abram's imagination, his free will, and the image of God. The writer also makes it possible for us to make the connection between Abram's creating an altar of metaphysical space and what unfolds in Genesis 1. On the second day, God creates an expanse within the abyss—an expanse of light and life and generativity. The expanse is called the heavens. The expanse is the basis for everything that God does as he creates the world. Then, on the fourth day, God creates additional expanses of light—the sun, the moon, and the stars—each of which constitutes an expanse within the first expanse of the heavens. On the fourth day, Genesis 1 portrays additional expanses of light and life within the first expanse of light and life. Notice the similarity between the expanses portrayed in Genesis 1 and Abram's actions: By building an altar, Abram creates a platform expanse of rock on which he enkindles fire in the place where his initial encounter with God comes to fulfillment as God actually appears to Abram. On the expanse of the altar, Abram enkindles a flame of fire. Metaphysically, the expanse of the heavens; the expanses of the sun, moon, and stars; the expanse of Abram's imagination, which is absorbed with God; and the fire upon the altar are all connected: each is a reflection, expression, and embodiment of the other. Together they form essential interconnections for Abram's imagination. The building of the altar establishes a metaphysical connection between Abram's experience with God and the creation of expanses of space in Genesis 1. Abram's altar involves the artistic embodiment of both his interaction with God who has led him and appeared to him and the creation of the expanse of the heavens, the source of light and life.

The altar is the embodiment of Abram's sustained encounter with God. I want to call that encounter *primary knowing*—a knowing that is completely active, engaged, and direct, as distinguished from knowledge that is a finished, but stagnant, object. Primary knowing is a way of characterizing Abram's relationship with God: it is direct, engaged, unfolding, alive, and sustained. The relationship is becoming rock solid (like the altar) as it inflames every aspect of Abram's life. This is why he builds an altar: it is the physical embodiment of a relationship with God that is both solid and aflame. Building an altar, Abram is formatting his relationship with God, a relationship where God has been leading him in his consciousness, on earth, and finally in appearing to Abram on the earth. The building of the altar creates an imaginative matrix in the form of a physical monument with which Abram can remember God, maintain his encounter with God, continue his conversation with God, reflect on God, and develop his understanding of God's dealings with both Abram and the world, as well as Abram's own dealings with God and the world that God created. Through his interaction with God at the altar, Abram can continue to develop his own understanding of the mystery of God's presence in both Abram's life and in the world. That understanding will involve the ongoing unfolding of a way of knowing God that is the primary presence of Abram's imagination and the way Abram lives, moves, and embodies the presence of mystery.

The altar—the expression of Abram's imagination—forms a matrix of Abram's creativity, which in turn becomes a source of deeper knowing.

MATRIX OF CREATIVITY

The field of the finite is all that we can see, hear, touch, remember, and describe. This field is basically that which is manifest, or tangible. The essential quality of the infinite, by contrast, is its subtlety, its intangibility. This quality is conveyed in the word spirit, whose root meaning is "wind or breath." This suggests an invisible but pervasive energy to which the manifest world of the finite responds. This energy, or spirit, infuses all living beings, and without it any organism must fall apart into its constituent elements. That which is truly alive in the living being is this energy of spirit, and this is never born and never dies.
—David Bohm quoted in Joseph Jaworski, *Source*

A s I reflected on the seemingly endless mystery Genesis 1 embodies, I began to realize that the story establishes a matrix of creativity in which we can both know God and engage our own imaginations and creativity. As a matrix of creativity, Genesis 1 provides an ongoing source of ongoing knowing, or, in the words of Louise Cowen, a lightning rod for knowing and understanding.

Another way to put this: one of the foundational insights of Genesis 1 is that we are created in the image of God. At the core of our humanity are imagination and the capacity for creativity. One—but by no means the only—way to see Genesis 1 involves understanding the creative process. It begins on "Day 1" with an awareness of formlessness, chaos, and the ominous threat of the abyss. There is either nothingness or mere substance. God embodies awareness: his spirit hovers, his breath blows over the formless abyss. God then initiates the processes of creativity with the words, "Let there be light." These words address, define, and bring the first inklings of clarity to the entire situation. The words, "Let there be light," express a reality that is of a different kind than the dark. God is aware of dark, meaningless, formlessness. This awareness involves a primary knowing on God's part: dark, fathomless, formlessness is neither desirable nor acceptable. A thoughtful word from the imagination and will of God with complete foresight establishes conditions in which creativity can unfold: light, breath, and the awareness of the current reality of formlessness define the undesirability of the current reality as they create the initial conditions in which reality of a completely different kind can now emerge and unfold. The new conditions allow us to imagine how light, breath, and awareness can lead to creativity, new ends, and a new world. The light makes us witnesses to the formless abyss, even as it allows us to imagine new possibilities. And the breath of God allows us to imagine where we can go and what we might do with our capacity for drinking orderliness and acting on our imaginations. Breath and light are the signs and embodiment of hope for new creation in the midst of chaos.

New creation begins to emerge on "Day 2." God first imagines an expanse of light and life and generativity. God then speaks, and his word and action create an opening in the midst of the abyss, which develops into a vast expanse of light and life and generativity. The vast expanse is the fruit of forethought. What begins as a tiny opening expands into an un-quantifiable heaven. The expanse is of a completely different kind than the abyss. And yet, the expanse creates conditions, including order, light, and generativity, in which the substance of the abyss becomes useful as elements for the germination, development, and growth of life. The introduction of the expanse within the chaos transforms the abyss into a treasure as it comes to provide elements and material for creation.

Just as the initiation of creation involves the separation of light from darkness and the creation of the expanse, so on "Day 3" does God bring forth an expanse of earth by separating the land from the waters, rendering the expanse of land a source of life. God then plants seed beneath the surface of the land, which, when in contact with water, germinates, and slowly, but steadily puts forth roots which drink in nutrients and create an essential relationship of symbiosis between the seed, land, nutrients and water. Above the surface of the land, it will not appear that anything is happening; but beneath the surface, an entire system of symbiosis and rootedness unfolds, creating the metabolic conditions in which life can emerge from the earth, develop, grow, and come to fruition, which produces additional seed, which gives birth to additional germination and life.

On "Day 4," God creates expanses of light and life within the expanse of the heavens. Expanses within the expanse create the conditions in which creativity, by becoming the norm, gains momentum: God is creating sources of generativity within the Source of Generativity—the matrix of creation. The abyss of chaos is no longer ominous; it no longer threatens: sources of light and life within life and light have become normative. Conditions and precedents for creativity are now in place, and the stuff of the abyss is now the substance of rootedness, nutrients, germination, and metabolism—in a word, a matrix of development and growth. What once was threat is now resource. What once was dead is now a source of life. What once was isolation is now in connection. What once was inert is now in motion. The conditions are now established not only for hope and momentum, but also for conversation and dialogue. "Day 7" is a day of rest. It allows us to relax the grip of intensity that is part and parcel to the momentum of the creative process. It allows us to look back on both objects and subjects of our creativity for the sheer joy of observing. And what is there to observe? Perhaps we might first notice that the world begins as a transfiguration. In Genesis 1, we see what the actions of creation look like, and we see what happens to the substance of the abyss as it is transformed into a world—a meaningful whole. When it comes to creative processes, transfiguration is the norm. On Day 7, we have the opportunity to reflect: as humans created in the image of God, we, like God, are vehicles of transfiguration. The transfiguration begins in the inklings and intuitions of human imagination, where we take in pre-figured circumstances and substances that are at best in chaos, and worse, threaten as only a formless abyss can, and begin to open ourselves to the first inklings and intuitions of new possibilities and forms of life and togetherness. In rest, we can begin to open our imaginations to new alternatives to current undesirable, if not unacceptable, circumstances. As we do so, we discover that imaginations opened become magnets for alternatives and lenses for the recognition of small, but distinct, openings of creativity and hope. Awakening from sleep, we begin opening our eyes to the opening of opportunities that we might otherwise miss.

As matrix of creativity, Genesis 1 opens our eyes so that we can recognize humans in the image of God as creator of a *whole* world. Like God, we have the capacity for awareness of the totality, which is what Genesis 1 as matrix of creativity accomplishes in us—that is, in our imaginations. As humans, we have the capacity for awareness of the totality. As the image of God, we have been created with an inner drive towards creativity. The story reminds us of this inner drive. It also broadens our awareness that we live and move and have our being in a world that is created whole, the wholeness of which is reconstructed and renewed in and through our own creativity. The story reminds us of this awareness. This is important because in our focus on the demands of everyday living, we are wont to lose our awareness of the whole, including the creative process. The matrix of creativity serves as a frequent reminder of both the meaning and direction of the created world in its wholeness. The matrix of creativity reminds us of both our essentiality as creators and our essential place in the creative matrix. The matrix reminds us of the relationship between imagination, forethought, and meaningful action. The matrix reminds us of the essentiality of relationships for the wholeness of the created order. The matrix allows us to sustain awareness and participation within a meaningful whole, which enjoys even greater development and completion in concert with our reflected action. The matrix of creativity knits the world—both substance and thought—into a meaningful web of unbroken wholeness. We find and exercise our places in the metaphysical expanse of generativity as we act on the fruits of our imaginations.

Genesis 1 embodies a matrix of creativity, which is conceived and comes to fruition in our imaginations. The matrix provides a living framework in which knowing, understanding, and creativity emerge and unfold. This matrix is at once a living framework in which we participate. This participation is one essential aspect of primary knowing. Fully engaged, we become creators. So doing, we take responsibility for our birthright and become fully human.

COMMUNION WITH THE EXPANSE

Lee and the others understood this to connote Bohm's view of a generative or creative order lying at the heart of the universe—a participatory universe. In such a universe, communion and fellowship are natural features of the topography, and intrinsic human warmth is common currency, part of the shared meaning of nature and society. Bohm felt the mind/body continuum ("You have to think with your whole body," he said to me) is concretely related to the deepest orders of the universe. If this is so, Lee said, then a change of meaning and purpose may open us to these orders, glimpsing a larger, perhaps very different universe.

—Joseph Jaworski, *Source*

For more than a decade, I have had the pleasure of visiting the Cathedral of Chartres in France. It is one of the treasures of the world. It was built in twelfth and thirteenth centuries. It contains over 170 stained glass windows and numerous sculptures, all of which portray some aspect of the story of God's involvement with the world. I remember the first time I visited the Cathedral and met Malcolm Miller, who has published one of the finest books on the Cathedral. He pointed out that the windows and sculptures were all created prior to the invention of the printing press (Johannes Gutenberg invented the press in 1450). This meant that most of the people who visited and worshiped in the Cathedral were illiterate. Stories from the Bible are the subjects of most sculptures and stained glass windows. Among other things, this meant that the Cathedral served as a kind of living medieval library, with which the priests of the church could teach stories from the Bible.

The things that impress and move me about the Cathedral of Chartres are too many to list in a short essay. Two matters are especially relevant here. The first is the architectural coherence and wholeness of the Cathedral. The Cathedral has something in common with the writings of St. Thomas of Aquinas, and that something is comprehensiveness. One of St. Thomas's goals was to write about everything that matters. He sought in his writings to write of theology in its wholeness. One of his most important writings is the *Summa Theologica*, in which St. Thomas tries to touch on every essential matter of theology. The Cathedral of Chartres is like St. Thomas' *Summa* in that it is the architectural and artistic creation of a whole world. It is a world filled with light. The light, coming through the stained glass windows, which portray God's involvement with the world, bathe the walls of the Cathedral in an artist's palette of color. The Cathedral is also an architectural unity. Everything is related to everything. Nothing is out of place. Twentieth century quantum physicist David Bohm spoke and wrote of the *unbroken wholeness of the implicate order of the universe*. What David Bohm said about the nature of the universe at the quantum level can also be said about the architectural and artistic relationships within the Cathedral of Chartres. Each part of the Cathedral is connected to the whole. By nature of design, the Cathedral is a world of unbroken wholeness. Although it is not possible for one person to be mindful of each part at

One of the things that make Abraham remarkable is that Abraham's faith did not consist of mere trust or blind obedience. His faith came to have substance that unfolded in his interactions with God. It told a story. Abraham's faith came to embody the ways in which God works in the world. This knowledge begins to develop in earnest with Abraham's getting his head, so to speak, into the expanse of the heavens. What develops in Abraham is a primary knowing—an understanding of God and God's involvement with the world that is both real and present and yet to unfold.

From the time that Abram (his name isn't lengthened until the seventeenth chapter of Genesis) first responds to the voice of God through the time that Abram builds his first altar, everything that Abram does in response to God is completely admirable. It was not long, however, before Abram was off in search of food. There was famine in Canaan, and Abram went to Egypt hoping to be able to feed his family. This time, Abram was led not so much by the voice and direction of God, but by his appetite. I do not intend this as a criticism of Abram. I can easily imagine myself doing the same thing, especially if it were a matter of providing food for my family. I can also easily imagine Abram's lack of courage when it came to facing the Egyptians. Recognizing that his wife Sarai was beautiful, Abram asked her to pose as his sister. This allowed Abram to save his own skin by selling his wife into Pharaoh's harem, which is exactly what Abram did. This resulted in a physical relationship between Pharaoh and Sarai. It also resulted in Pharaoh's reaping plagues. Sometimes when my students read this, the story offends their sense of justice: Abram is the one who is lying, but Pharaoh is the one who gets socked with the plague. This almost always provokes students to ask, "What's up with that?" I can fully appreciate their incredulity. What I try to do in these circumstances is to help them to understand the perspective of the writer: Abram and Sarai were husband and wife, and when Sarai became a member of Pharaoh's harem, Pharaoh's relationship with Sarai was adulterous. This constituted a rupture in the fabric of the order of the universe. The symptom of the rupture was the plague. As embodied in the story, the relationship of husband and wife was essential to the fabric of the universe, and adultery ruptured the fabric.

The plague is Pharaoh's clue that he has caused such a rupture. He may not have *realized* that his relationship with Sarai was a problem, but the violation of the order of the fabric of life was real nonetheless. The consequences were real. To his credit, Pharaoh responded to the knowledge of what he had done by restoring Sarai to her husband Abram. Pharaoh also made Abram into a wealthy man.

To say that Abram's conduct in Egypt was not one of his better performances is an understatement. Abram's behavior was duplicitous and cowardly. So why does the writer include conduct that is so blatantly un-exemplary? Among other things, the book of Genesis is showing us the development of Abram's faith. The development of primary knowing of God and God's involvement with the world takes time. It is a long and involved process. There is little about it that is easy. Learning that matters is learning that takes time—especially when the subject of learning encompasses something as important as knowing the mystery in which God works in the world.

When does Abram begin to get things right? In Genesis 15, Abram has an encounter with God. The story begins with God's telling Abram that God is Abram's shield and protector. Abram believes that his protection and security will come from having a family, so Abram, wondering how this will unfold, reminds God that he (Abram) has no son. Moreover, his heir is a slave, Eliezer of Damascus. God responds by telling Abram that he will become the father of a child. God brings this understanding to fruition in Abram's imagination by taking him outside at night and directing his attention to the stars in the expanse of the heavens: "Count the stars if you are able. So shall the number of your descendants be." The writer tells us that Abram believed God and that God counted Abram's belief as righteousness.

What is unfolding in Abram's imagination is a knowing that is primary because it is direct. God answers Abram's question about descendants by bringing his imagination into communion with the expanse of the heavens—the generative order of the universe: God draws Abram's awareness and imagination into communion with the stars of the heavens. A communion of Abram's imagination with expanses within the expanse of the heavens is primary knowing. This constitutes a major step in the development of Abram's faith. Abram's understanding of God begins to progress as Abram cooperates with God, who draws Abram's imagination into communion with the generative order of the universe. Abram is on his way to knowing and understanding God.

This faith—this primary knowing—is, in the artwork of the Cathedral, present everywhere. In their design, the artists have emplaced Abram in strategic locations throughout the Cathedral. They have placed the father of primary knowing in multiple central locations. So doing, they have created the possibility for primary knowing in the multiple locals of our lives. Each is central. Wherever we happen to stand is a possible center of primary knowing—an opportunity for communion with God, the expanse of the heavens, and the generative order of the universe. There is no place that is not embedded, that does not contain primary generativity. The artists of the Cathedral knew this. We can know this as well.

With that is a word of hope. Like Abram, we have shortcomings. We make mistakes. We sin. We hurt loved ones, and we too often tear the very fabric of life. What matters is our sustained willingness to take responsibility and to learn. Abram did not allow himself to become consumed and debilitated by his mistakes, sins, and shortcomings. Abram discovered that communion with the expanse of the heavens and the generative order of the universe is an ever-present opportunity. It was for him; it is for us. When we open our hearts and imaginations in the Cathedral, it transforms us into witnesses.

ABRAM'S KNOWING

Human knowledge processing is not completely executed within the physiological brain. Rather, the brain is one neurologically localized utility that serves a much more extended individual "mind" or "consciousness."

—Joseph Jaworski, *Source*

The Cathedral of Chartres is a complete world. It is complete by design. Everything is in place for a particular reason. The architectural structure and the windows and sculptures are related to each other. By entering the Cathedral and giving it our full attention, it becomes possible for us to synchronize our imaginations with a world that is complete, with its various parts in sync. Remarkably, this is what Abram accomplishes in the fifteenth chapter of Genesis. In the first part of Genesis 15, Abram managed to get his head into the heavens: his imagination was in communion with the stars—each of which constitutes an expanse within the expanse of the heavens, which is also the seat of the generative order of the universe. Like with the expanse of the heavens, the Cathedral is a complete world that is teeming with far more meaning than any single person can keep in mind at any single moment in time. We cannot take it all in at once. We can, however, be *aware* that the Cathedral embodies far more meaning than we can bear at a particular moment in time. In other words, we can understand and appreciate that the Cathedral is a complete, complex world in which everything is coherently related.

In Genesis 15, Abram comes to an understanding of God that is complete. This doesn't mean that Abram's knowledge is exhaustive— that Abram knows everything about the mystery of God that there is to know. Completion isn't the same as exhaustiveness. Let me give a homey example: Every house that Nancy and I have lived in has been complete. But not all of the homes have been the same size or had identical features. A small house can still be a complete house, just as a short poem can still be a complete poem, or a short song a complete song. Completeness and exhaustiveness are independent variables. A sonnet by Shakespeare is just as complete as, say, a Shakespearean tragedy. In Genesis 15, Abram comes to a kind of *knowledge of God* that is complete. This knowledge stands at the heart of Abram's faith. His faith, in other words, includes his understanding of the mystery of God and God's dealings with the world. This knowledge involves both the present and the past. It also foreshadows the future. Abram's knowledge of God is developing. I believe that Abram's understanding of God is breathtaking. I am still stunned not only by what Abram saw, but also by the way—the manner—in which this understanding developed and unfolded in Abram.

The events that unfold in the fifteenth chapter of Genesis mark a watershed in the development of Abram's faith. Abram's encounter with God in Genesis 15 has two parts, which involve the answer to two different, complementary questions. The first we saw in the previous essay: the question that Abram posed to God involved the issues of Abram's descendants: *My wife and I are old—well beyond child-bearing years. How are we to know that we shall have descendants?* God answered this question by drawing Abram's attention into the expanse of the heavens, where Abram's imagination was in communion with the generative order of the universe. This was the genesis of Abram's faith, which involved a kind of knowledge of God and God's world. Abram was in communion with both.

The story in Genesis 15 continues with God's identifying himself as the one who brought Abram and his family to the land on which he now stands. Abram responds to God by posing a second question: "How am I to *know* that I will possess this land?" The kind of knowledge that Abram begins to develop is not a mere cognitive knowledge. In other words, it wasn't head knowledge. This knowledge didn't consist of mere information. It was "a knowing" that involved his entire being— including his body, his will, and his conduct— in communion with God. That knowledge in communion deepens in the interaction between Abram and God that follows. God responds to Abram's question, "How am I to *know* that I will possess this land?" by directing Abram to bring to God three animals and two birds. The animals are a heifer, a female goat, and a ram. The birds are a pigeon and a turtle dove. God directs Abram to slaughter the animals, divide the carcasses in two, and to lay each half over against the other.

This sacrifice is filled with mystery, which is ours to observe, unpack, interact with, and understand. What is there to observe? One of the first things that we notice is that the directions that God gives for Abram to execute begin with a voluntary act of de-creation: God instructs Abram to take animals, the fruit of creation, which are alive and complete, and to kill them—to violently take away their life—and to split them in two. The enactment of these directions would be of no small order. Nothing that God instructs Abram to do can be easy. The splitting of the carcasses would involve hard, laborious, gory labor. What God does is to require Abram to enter completely into an experience of de-creation, where he takes something that is good and full of life, to sacrifice it, and to split the carcasses in two. Once Abram has finished this action, Abram lays each half over against the other. The description of this action is ambiguous. Does it mean that the two halves of the carcasses are pressed together? Or does it mean that each half lies immediately opposite the other on the sacrificial altar? Either way, we know that by executing the killing and the splitting of the carcasses, Abram becomes the instrument of the taking of life. This experience is now his; the knowledge of execution and de-creation is primary, that is, first-hand.

The details that follow are intriguing and ultimately filled with meaning: birds of prey descend on the carcasses of the sacrifice. Abram responds by driving away the birds of prey. The sacrifice ends with a smoking fire pot and a flaming torch moving among the sacrificial carcasses.

So what does all of this mean? The key resides in a dream that Abram has in the middle of the execution of this sacrifice. After the descent of the birds of prey, which Abram drives away, Abram is overcome by sleep, during which he has a dream that fills him with dread and horror. In this dream, Abram learns that he will not only have descendants, but also that in four hundred years, his descendants will be enslaved in a foreign land. God, however, who is also the author of Abram's dream, will deliver Abram's descendants from slavery and bring them to the land on which Abram currently resides. This dream unfolds between Abram's driving away the birds of prey and the movement of the smoking fire pot and flaming torch between the pieces of the carcasses. The dream, of course, foreshadows the enslavement of the Hebrews in the Book of Exodus, along with God's calling Moses to deliver his people from slavery and ultimately leading them to the land where Abram resides. The dream provides the key to understanding the meaning of the sacrifice in which the dream is embedded and ultimately the contents of Abram's knowledge and faith. The dream shows us that the sacrifice tells the story of the enslavement of the Hebrews and the exodus from Egypt. This means that the carcasses of the animals play the same role in the sacrifice that the Hebrews play in Egypt: as slaves, they are "as good as dead." The birds of prey that descend on the carcasses play the role that Pharaoh and the Egyptian taskmasters play as they as they execute oppression on the Hebrews. And Abram, who drives away the birds of prey from the carcasses, plays the role of God and Moses, who deliver the Hebrews from slavery and oppression.

The meaning of the decent of the birds of prey on the carcasses may also point to the decent of the angel of death on the first-born of all living, with Abram's driving away the birds of prey foreshadowing the role of the blood on the doorposts and the lintel, which signals to the angel of death to pass over the homes of the Hebrews. In other words, this sacrifice bears the poetic capacity to embody more than one aspect of the life of the Hebrews in Egypt.

What, then, can we say of the role of the smoking fire pot and flaming torch that pass between the carcasses of the sacrificial animals? These objects that move within the sacrifice mysteriously prefigure the pillar of cloud by day and the pillar of fire by night that will lead the Hebrews out of Egypt in the exodus.

In coming to an understanding of the mystery and meaning of this sacrifice, it is important that we remember that the sacrifice and the dream that unfolds in the midst of the sacrifice are the answer to the question that Abram poses to God: *How am I to know that I shall possess this land?* The answer to the question is embodied in the sacrifice which Abram executes and in his imagination, in which a prophetic dream unfolds. The dream provides an opening in the unconscious sleep of Abram that brings to consciousness the meaning of the events surrounding Abram's dream. This allows us to observe that Abram's execution of the sacrifice embodies knowledge of the mystery of God's work with his people—a knowledge that is so far-reaching in relevance as to include the substance of the ways in which God will deliver his people from horrific circumstances that lie four hundred years in Abram's future. This knowledge is not a finished, static product, but an active and engaged knowing—a knowing that involves Abram's imagination and thought processes, to be sure. But it is not a knowing that is limited to Abram's thought processes—as incalculably important as they are. It is a knowing that actively embodies mystery—a mystery that is present in Abram as he is completely absorbed in the implementation of directives that God is giving him. It is a knowing that unfolds in Abram solely *because* he is completely drawn in to what God is directing him to do. Just as God creates an expanse of generative order on the second day of Creation, so here is an expanse of knowing the mystery of God that is unfolding in both Abram's imagination and actions as he diligently follows God's instructions.

THE KEY WINDOW

In reference to the Levite and the priest in the Parable of the Good Samaritan, you state, "By refusing to help, they also degraded themselves." I learned this lesson first from my father when I was very young. He was describing the attitudes of some of his fellow health care workers who would talk down to patients or provide poor care. He described to me how it was their privilege to serve. People give us a gift when they allow us to help them. They give us the chance to give our brief shadow of time on earth a purpose. When we view others as subservient, we only negate our own worth and rob ourselves of humanity.

—Meriah Moore

I found it to be the key to understanding the Cathedral of Chartres. It is the window that unlocked the mystery. It was as though the difficulties portrayed in one story in one time and one place were being responded to, answered, and resolved by another story that Jesus told in another time in another place. After spending many an hour living with these stories, I finally saw that the two stories interpenetrate one another. What is embodied, artistically, in The Good Samaritan and Adam and Eve Window in the Cathedral of Chartres is that delectation of mystery that Claude Tresmontant describes in his book on the metaphysics of the Hebrews:

> Mystery today means something impenetrable to the mind, something never to be understood. To St. Paul and the early Christian thinkers it was on the contrary the particular object of intelligence, its fullest nourishment. The *musterion* is something so rich in intelligible content, so inexhaustibly full of delectation for the mind that no contemplation can ever reach its end. It is an eternal delectation of the mind.

This is what the Cathedral of Chartres is to me: *an eternal delectation of the mind*. But this is not so for any reason that is in any way superficial. The Cathedral draws us into a knowing that is primary and inexhaustible. It is a world of wonder.

It was over a dozen years ago that I first heard Malcolm Miller describe how to "read" a stained glass window. He used, as his example, "The Good Samaritan and Adam and Eve Window." This window was created in the 13th century—some two hundred years prior to Gutenberg's invention of the printing press. Among other things, the windows in the Cathedral formed a kind of biblical library for people who were illiterate. The priests of the cathedral could point to the windows and use these works of art to tell the story and to cultivate understanding. For me personally, the Cathedral of Chartres is the complement to my other favorite place in Europe, Gladstone's Library in Wales. Whereas the Cathedral is a "library of art"—windows, sculptures, and architecture—Gladstone's Library is a residential library of books, the legacy of England's most theologically-minded prime minister.

There were two essential matters that I learned from Mr. Miller on that fortunate day. The first is that one "reads" the window from left to right and from the bottom to the top. The second was that the Parable of the Good Samaritan and the story of Adam and Eve in the Garden of Eden were, in the artistic design of the window, connected to each other. Subsequent to my first visit to the Cathedral, I began to ask, what do these two stories have to do with each other? What insight led the creators of this astonishing window to place these two stories side by side? How are they connected? In what sense does one story resolve the other?

Finding answers was not, as we are wont to say, "rocket-science." The keys are of course both simple and "right in front of our eyes." One of the beauties of these windows is that they conceal nothing: the meaning is present for all to see. What I did was simple: I placed the episodes of the two stories side by side, in my journal. What I wrote looked like this:

Parable of the Good Samaritan	Adam, Eve, and the Garden of Eden
A man is going from Jerusalem to Jericho	Adam and Eve are exiled from the Garden of Eden
Robbers attack the man, beat him, and leave him half dead	Adam and Eve take the forbidden fruit Cain kills Abel
The priest and the Levite cross to the other side of the road without helping the man	The serpent tempts Eve Cain envies Abel when God accepts his offering
The Samaritan has compassion for the man	Adam chokes on the fruit
The Samaritan places the wounded man in the inn	Adam and Eve are placed in the Garden of Eden
Who is my neighbor?	Am I my brother's keeper?
Who proved to be neighbor to the man in need?	Eve is created from the rib of Adam

I developed this chart by taking the episodes portrayed in the Cathedral window, supplemented by a couple of things that the Bible portrays that scenes in the window may imply, and then seeking to identify connections between the two stories. There are lots of important connections to be made. I made the connections both by reflecting on the windows and from reading the texts in Genesis 3–4 and Luke 10.

What I first noticed was that in some respects, the two stories are inverted images of each other. As I looked for relationships, I noticed that the Parable of the Good Samaritan portrays components that are connected to the complementary episodes from Genesis in reverse order. There are a couple of exceptions to this as the inversion of the stories was not a conscious, deliberately mechanical process of artistic ordering. Still, the two stories remarkably mirror each other as inversions.

I next noticed that the two questions asked in Genesis and Luke provide essential connections between the stories. Immediately prior to Jesus's telling of the Parable of the Good Samaritan in the Gospel of Luke, a lawyer asks Jesus, "Who is my neighbor?" The Parable is Jesus's answer to the lawyer's question. In Genesis 4, Cain asks a question that is of the same kind as the question that the lawyer asks Jesus: "Am I my brother's keeper?" Both questions point to an affinity that humans share that both lies at the heart of our humanity and also obligates us one to another for a reasonable measure of helpfulness.

After completing his telling of the Parable, Jesus asks the lawyer, "Who proved to be neighbor to the person in need?"

The lawyer of course pointed to the actions of the Samaritan, whose actions were neighborly because they were hospitable.

Jesus responded by saying, "Go and do likewise."

One of the things we notice about these statements when we look at the chart is that the question of who *proved* to be neighbor to the man in need lines up with Eve's being created from the rib of Adam, which is portrayed in the Window. The creation of Eve and the connection between her creation and the Samaritan's proving to be neighbor in his actions convey an insight into our common humanity. That insight involves the recognition that our common humanity is inherent and unqualified. We are connected to one another and those connections involve our dignity as humans.

For those of us who have enjoyed long life with the Parable of the Good Samaritan, it is difficult to remember just how much enmity poisoned the relationship between Samaritans and Jews. We have in our own experience living examples of the kinds of charged feelings that would have accompanied Jesus's telling of the Parable. We need merely consider tensions that exist between some Palestinians and some Israelis to this day to get a sense of the climate of feeling in which the Parable would have been experienced. Against the backdrop of these charged feelings we can recognize that what makes the Samaritan good involves his willingness to see through a venomous smog thick with hostilities to the actual humanity of the man lying on the ground before him. We see a man who has the unconditional feeling that he is called upon to help—to take action, to do something for—the person lying wounded before him. The Samaritan does something that the priest, Levite, and Cain were unwilling to do, and that is to look upon a human being as a human being. They were unwilling to recognize the reality that was both present and clear, along with their insoluble connection to that reality.

What we see is that the priest and the Levite, in their refusal to help the man in need whom they encountered, not only betrayed the humanity of the person they refused to help, but they betrayed their own inner call to respond to the legitimate need that they encountered, which they possessed the power to resolve. By refusing to help, they also degraded themselves. The solution to the problem of our betraying ourselves as we betray others manifests itself as we observe the two stories together.

When we see these stories side-by-side, both in the window and in the chart I prepared in my journal, a larger meaning begins to emerge. This meaning unfolds in the relationship between the two stories, which, taken together, form an interconnected whole. This interconnected whole precipitates and embodies the kind of mystery that Tresmontant identifies as "an eternal delectation of the mind." There are two keys to understanding this mystery. *The first is to recognize that meaning and mystery are embodied in the interconnected whole.* The Window helps us to recognize that when Jesus told the Parable of the Good Samaritan, deep was calling unto deep. The realities that the Parable bears call to and resolve the realities that Genesis 3 and 4 portray. As we become willing to know and to understand the realities that form the interconnected whole, and as we allow ourselves to resonate with the feelings and actions of the Samaritan, we enter the world of primary knowing.

The second key to understanding this mystery involves our ability to see each other as human beings and to respond to one another's humanity with love. Every time another person's humanity calls upon ours, we are called into the world of primary knowing—a place where our common humanity is connected. Every time we act on that feeling, we enter the world of primary knowing. When we act on the feeling that another person's humanity calls upon our own humanity, we enter the world of knowable mystery, the world of primary knowing. In our willingness to take action, the generative order of the universe—the presence of grace—heals our self-betrayal as we respond as agents of healing in love. This opens the flood gates for our own cleansing from sin, bringing us to greater and greater wholeness. We not only re-establish interconnections in which we play essential roles; we know it. This act of knowing is whole.

The Faith of Abraham

*On the left side of the U, we wrote "Observe, observe, observe."
At the bottom of the U, we wrote "Go to that place of deeper
knowing." And on the right side of the U: "Act swiftly in flow."*

*In order to enable the collapse of boundaries between self, others,
and the universe, one or a collective must unambiguously stand
in a place of love, caring, and sacrifice for others—for the whole
system under investigation. It is at this moment of oneness that the
participants are acting out of the unfolding generative order—the
unbroken wholeness from which seemingly discrete events take
place. And it is at this moment that new realities are enacted for the
benefit of the whole system. This is why the advanced U-process is so
powerful. It is designed to serve life. The process itself is a volitional
act of love, enabling new realities.*

—Joseph Jaworski, *Source*

There were aspects of going to seminary that were intoxicating.
I was studying matters of great importance with incredibly
clever people. My professors were learned, eloquent, and

filled with all kinds of passion. Some of what they were teaching us I understood. Even when I did not understand, I sensed that what I did not yet understand was well worth patient pursuit. At the time, the Claremont School of Theology was attracting scholars who were leaders in their fields. The breadth of their learning was staggering. They took an interest in me, they answered my questions, and they led me to books that, if they didn't fully change my life, certainly formed and transformed the ways I looked at the world, especially the world of the Bible.

One of those books was by the French structuralist anthropologist, Claude Lévi-Strauss. He had devised an algebraic formula that he claimed described the unconscious structure of the human mind. At the time, I was good with algebra (I was the kind of guy who took calculus as an elective). Figuring out how Lévi-Strauss derived his formula wasn't easy, but I stayed with it, and eventually I was able to understand it. I also started applying the formula to everything I looked at and everything I read, including the Bible. This made it possible for me to develop models for explaining all matters biblical. My ideas were coherent. My professors liked them. And I was becoming mighty impressed with myself. For the first time in my life, I was intoxicated with the new wine of learning, and I think it safe to say that I was a fresh wineskin.

But it wasn't long before someone asked me a question that I could not answer. This was a humbling, if not humiliating, experience. I was teaching a class on Genesis in a church. Not only was I impressed with myself, but others expressed awe over the quality of my learning, and that confirmed my illusion that I had it all together. We were studying Genesis 22, the story of Abraham's near-sacrifice of Isaac. A man in the class, who was probably in his late fifties, said that it was difficult for him to be impressed with Abraham. I asked why this was so. The man said that if Abraham were a man of courage, when God asked him to sacrifice his son, Abraham should have offered his own life in Isaac's stead.

This was a difficult challenge for a young man who wanted to electrify people with his knowledge. The truth is that when the man asked his question, I was embarrassed. I was also short on wisdom because I was short on experience and humility. There were acres of biblical insight that I had yet to glean (there still are) because I was viewing the Bible through the lens of an anthropologist's formula instead of seeking insight on its own terms. Sadly, I was so taken with myself that I presumed the blinders that I wore to be fashionable. In retrospect, I can see that my blinders fit a manner of thinking that confused knowledge derived from a narrow world view with wisdom, the fruit of hard-earned reflection on interconnected experience, consequences, and the possibilities of goodness aforethought. Sadly, I would relinquish my blinders with a reluctance born of stubbornness to which I was militantly blind. Happily, reluctance was impeachable and finally lost its grip on the throne of my sense of self-importance. But because of my reluctance, fueled by a pride that was venomous, it would be years before I would welcome insight from the Abraham story on its own terms. In the meantime, instead of casting my net into the deep of Abraham's story, I would for the most part ignore him. I am in no way proud to admit this, but it is the truth. Instead of letting the stories of Abraham speak for themselves, I sentenced them to solitary confinement. Sadly, I adopted the presumption that Abraham, when it came to his relationship with Isaac, was a coward.

There have been well-meaning believers who have, with good intention, presumed that to study the Bible *as literature* involved objectifying its meaning and insight and holding it at arm's length, if not complete detachment. Because the Bible is literature, I found that approaching it as such allowed the stories to convey their own insight into both God and mystery on their own terms. I began to see, in my own reading, that this approach began to yield, at first, a pearl or two. This led eventually to whole treasure stores that could not be exhausted.

I cannot identify a single moment when I began to realize that sustained observation of the story would lead to the recognition of interconnected wholes, but for reasons I can't entirely explain, I found the grace to observe Abraham—merely to observe. I did feel an inner movement of spirit to stay with him, to linger. There was a pull. Something was drawing me in. At first, merely sitting with the Abraham story wasn't easy. I am a fidget. There are times I can get to that place of inner knowing, and then, for reasons for which I am sure I am entirely responsible, they leave me; or I leave them. But I sensed Abraham too important for failure provoked by my unwillingness. I was willing. I wanted to see. Thankfully, there are times in which willingness is all that is required. Miraculously, I was getting ready to know the Abraham story on its own terms.

This in no way meant that I could ignore the gravity of human sacrifice. I recently spent a couple of days in the Louvre in Paris. I sat in a room devoted to the paintings of Nicolas Poussin. I was especially stunned by his painting, entitled, "The Judgment of Solomon" (1653). Two women are before King Solomon, who sits on his throne. One of the women had rolled over on her infant son during the night and unintentionally killed him. This woman, seeing the loss of her own baby, switched it with the infant of another woman. The woman whose son was alive awoke in the morning to find the dead baby, which, on closer examination, she noticed wasn't hers. The woman whose baby had been taken from her sought justice from King Solomon. Both women claimed the child who was alive to be her own. Solomon demonstrated his wisdom by ordering that a sword be used to divide the living child in two so that one half could be given to each of the two mothers who claimed him to be her own. The true mother, of course, pled for the sparing of the life of her child, relinquishing her rights to the false claimant. This allowed Solomon to recognize the full nature of the circumstances for which he was called to adjudicate, enabling him to find for the true mother and her son.

In Poussin's painting, the face of the woman who lied about the children is possessed by a countenance of militant, envious hatred. Poussin has captured the woman's concern for no one but herself. For others, this woman could not care less. In the countenance and manner of the true mother of the living child, we witness panic born of sheer desperation. A longing for the preservation of his life supersedes even her longing to be with him. King Solomon's face conveys a quality of seriousness and concentration that meet the grave demand for critical discernment of both circumstances and claims.

As we take the time necessary to observe, the painting evokes an awareness in the viewer that cruelty to children (or to anything, for that matter) is not only wrong, but the wrongness is absolute. Poussin's painting evokes many feelings at once, including profound sadness over the loss of one child, revulsion and horror over the idea of sacrificing an innocent child, and awe over King Solomon's wisdom and presence of mind. The feeling and insight that Nicolas Poussin evokes help me sustain the inner climate and coherence in which to understand the Abraham story with a sufficient measure of clarity. From the perspective of a father who loves his son, what God calls Abraham to do is nothing short of horrific. I am certain I could not do this. If God called me to sacrifice my son or daughter, I hope, trust, and pray that the very least I would do would be to offer myself in their stead. I certainly could not live with myself were I to fail to do so.

Once God had called upon Abraham to prove his faith—to put it to the test—there is nothing else that Abraham could have thought about as he carried the fire and the knife as they made their three days journey to Mount Moriah. More than palpable, Abraham's thoughts and feelings would have throbbed. What kind of conversation could Abraham possibly have engaged in? The test of his faith would have obsessed every thought, every feeling, every motive, and every fiber of his will-power. Nothing else could have mattered—not in the way that the call to sacrifice his son mattered. This was the call to sacrifice *the son whom he loved*—a son for whom Abraham, in his deepest humanity, was completely responsible. Isaac was not only the source of endless joy and laughter; he was the gift of Abraham's deepest longing. Abraham was being called upon to sacrifice the fruit of his love.

Love, of course, is what qualifies this test as sacrifice. The ritual killing of his son Isaac could not be counted as sacrifice if Abraham's feeling for his son involved anything short of love. Without loving his son as completely as a father was capable, the killing of his son could not be reckoned as anything other than murder or atrocity. I will never forget the first time I saw the movie *Sophie's Choice*, directed by Alan J. Pakula, based on the story by William Styron. The circumstances of Sophie—mother and protector of two children, a son and a daughter whom Sophie loved—were nothing short of impossible. In a death camp, a Nazi guard demands that Sophie choose between the lives of her two children. He will take one to the gas chamber. Sophie must choose which will die and which will live. The circumstances are horrific. The mother loves both of her children equally and absolutely. And yet, if she doesn't make the choice—on the spot, with no time for reflection or improvisation—she stands to lose both. The choice that Sophie must make is far more than I can take in. And I can't help but feel that the feelings that we witness in Sophie convey something of the force of feeling that saturated every fragment of Abraham's consciousness. Nor can I imagine a situation more dire.

The circumstances that *Sophie's Choice* describes are not mere fiction. Nicholas D. Kristof was recently in Syria visiting a refugee camp. He met a middle-aged woman named Fawzia, a mother of two, who recently faced the same tragic choice as Sophie. Fawzia's family suffered through a shelling of the neighborhood in which she lived. Her eight-year-old son disappeared. At the same time, Fawzia and her other two children were in danger. She had to choose between staying, searching for her beloved son Mustafa, or taking her other two children and fleeing for their safety. Fawzia chose to protect her two remaining children, hoping to save them. When Nicholas Kristof met her, he of course found a mother who is "racked by guilt." How could she otherwise be? Fawzia's circumstances are gut-wrenching and horrific.

I can't help but realize that these are the kinds of feelings that would have weighed on Abraham. When God put Abraham to the test, the test could not but consume him completely.

As I try, feebly, to open my heart to at least some of the force of Abraham's circumstances, I must also own a personal dissatisfaction with the idea that the story of the near sacrifice of Isaac is the story of mere, blind obedience. I believe faith in general and the faith of Abraham in particular to be of a kind of importance that cannot be calculated in any kind of quantifiable terms. I am in awe of both Abraham and his faith. I hope and pray that I shall acquire a measure of that faith that is right for the life it is my privilege to live. That being said, I do not believe that faith is blind or that developing faith involves a series of exercises in militant ignorance. That Abraham obeyed God is beyond dispute and admirable—given a larger picture, which Genesis unfolds right before our eyes. But I am in no way convinced that the story of Abraham is the story of blind obedience any more than I am convinced that because Abraham did not offer himself in Isaac's stead, the story merits being shelved in a third-rate museum as a cheap relic of primitive curiosities. Obedience is too often demanded by those who want to maintain the illusion of their own superiority, if not their own power, and the demand for obedience is almost always placed on those the leader wishes to dominate. I do not believe that ideological martial law or interpretive totalitarianism leads to knowing God any more than I can accept totalitarian skepticism as a pathway to understanding.

What I find remarkable in trying to understand the Abraham story on its own terms is that it not only has the capacity to take us to that place of deeper knowing, but if we will stay with it (a challenge that is anything but easy), it will also take us to a place of knowing that is at once comprehendible and comprehensive. The comprehensive capacity of this story lies in the interconnections it brings to fruition when read in light of the complete story of Abraham in Genesis and then the story of Moses and the Hebrews in Exodus. The connections began to emerge in my own imagination when its link to the sacrifice in Genesis 15 presented itself. For what we can notice, if we place the two stories side-by-side, is that they are connected as inverse reflections of one another.

Abraham's Two Sacrifices

Genesis 15:7–16	Genesis 22:1–19
"How am I to know that I will inherit the land?"	"Because you have not withheld your son, you will inherit the land."
"Bring me animals and sacrifice them."	Abraham sacrifices the ram, which is caught in the thicket.
Abram drove away the birds of prey	"Do not lay your hand on your son."
Dream: the enslavement of Abram's descendants and their deliverance	Abraham binds Isaac. "Where is the lamb for the sacrifice?"
Smoking fire pot and flaming torch	Abraham carries the fire and knife
"To your descendants I will give the land."	"Take your only son Isaac, whom you love, and sacrifice him."

When we examined the sacrifice in Genesis 15, we discovered that the story of the sacrifice that Abram executes is connected to the Egyptian enslavement of the Hebrews in the book of Exodus. We made this discovery by connecting the actions of the sacrifice with Abram's dream. That showed us that the sacrifice that Abram implements embodies and prefigures the circumstances in which his descendants will find themselves. Like the split carcasses of the sacrifice, the slaves will be "as good as dead." Just at the birds of prey descend on the carcasses, so will Pharaoh and the task masters treat the slaves harshly, with brutality. And just as Abram drives away the birds of prey, so will Moses and God deliver the Hebrews from the horrific conditions of slavery in a foreign land. Just as the smoking fire pot and flaming torch move between the pieces of the sacrificial carcasses, so will God lead the Hebrews out of slavery and Egypt by means of a pillar of cloud by day and a pillar of fire by night. What we saw was that the sacrifice, which is connected to Abram's dream, constitutes a form of knowing that is so far-reaching that it foreshadows the future involvement of God with his people. This form of knowing embodies both the nature of God's power and also God's connections with his people and the world. The interest of this power centers on justice and deliverance. It seeks to capacitate God's people to take responsibility for the establishment of the connections of mutual justice and righteousness.

When we place these two stories of sacrifice side-by-side, we notice not only that they are inverted images of each other, but we can also notice their interconnections form a larger picture of the circumstances that Abraham's descendants will face. These connections prefigure God's power in delivering his people from slavery. The sacrifice in Genesis 15 is the response to the question Abram poses to God: "How am I to know that I will inherit the land?" The answer to this critical question is provided at the end of the near-sacrifice of Isaac: "Because you have not withheld your son, you will have offspring, and you will inherit the land." This is the answer to the paradox that the juxtaposition of the stories shows at the bottom of the chart: At the beginning of the story in Genesis 22, God says to Abraham, "Take your only son Isaac, whom you love, and sacrifice him." It is in connection with the end of the sacrifice in Genesis 15 that we see the paradox: "To your descendants I will give the land." God's directing Abram to bring animals and to sacrifice them in Genesis 15 is connected to the ram caught in the thicket, which Abraham sacrifices. Taken together, these interconnected parts prefigure the sacrifice of the Passover lamb, with its blood that will be smeared on the doorposts and the lintel of the houses of the Hebrews. Abram's driving away the birds of prey from the split carcasses is connected to the angel's telling Abraham, "Do not lay a hand on your son." The dread and horror of Abram's dream of slavery in Genesis 15 is connected with the horror that we feel when Abraham binds Isaac, who has asked his father, "Where is the lamb for the sacrifice," and places Isaac on the altar in Genesis 22. And the smoking fire pot and the flaming torch of Genesis 15 are connected with Abraham's carrying the fire and the knife in Genesis 22. In their connection, the fire and knife as instruments of sacrifice are transfigured into the pillar of cloud and fire of deliverance and salvation from slavery and oppression.

Notice how the book of Genesis establishes the literary connections that are the fruit of our willingness to observe. The dream of Abram in Genesis 15 is connected to the sacrifice he is prosecuting. Taken together, the dream and the sacrifice are connected to the enslavement of the Hebrews and their deliverance in the book of Exodus. Abraham's near sacrifice of Isaac is connected to the sacrifice Abram completes in Genesis 15. From this we learn that the story of Abraham's call to sacrifice his son embodies something of the horrors of the enslavement of the Hebrews along with the mystery of God's delivering them from slavery—the essential interconnections which constitute the Hebrews as people of God. The fact that Abraham suffers the horrors of the specter of sacrificing his only son Isaac whom he loves makes it possible for us, with Abraham, to know in our imaginations something of the horror and heartbreak of mothers and fathers of children in slavery. The story, in its capacity to shock us (and what can be more shocking than the call to sacrifice one's own child), makes possible an understanding of the dread of slavery to unfold in our imaginations as long as we will have a stomach for it. With this kind of knowing, we also see the wonder of God's involvement with his people in this impossible, heartbreaking, horrific situation. Just as in the story of the sacrifice of Isaac, the angel says to Abraham, "Do not lay your hand on the boy; for now I know that you fear God," and just as there is a ram caught in the thicket, which will be sacrificed in Isaac's stead, so will God direct the Hebrews to sacrifice a Passover lamb, which will make it possible for the firstborn children of the Hebrews to have their lives spared so that they can be delivered from slavery. Just as Isaac, the firstborn son of Sarah, is spared, so will be the children of Israel. They will finally be delivered from Egypt with their lives secure.

For Abraham, the near-sacrifice of Isaac involves a knowing. Whereas the sacrifice of the animals in Genesis 15 tells the story of the enslavement and deliverance of the Hebrews, the near-sacrifice of Isaac in Genesis 22 tells the same story, but in reverse order. The story of God's deliverance of Abraham's descendants is embedded in Abraham's faith. It forms the substance of his faith. Abraham's faith involves a knowing that is completely embodied in Abraham's life, actions, and interactions. In his interactions with God, Isaac, and sacrifice, Abraham dramatizes and embodies the circumstances that his descendants will face, along with their deliverance from those circumstances. Just as Isaac is bound and placed on the altar, so will the Hebrews be enslaved in Egypt. Just as the angel directs Abraham to release Isaac from the altar and to offer the ram in Isaac's stead, so will the angel of death pass over the homes of the Hebrews who sacrifice the Passover lamb. The substance of Abraham's faith consists of contents which Abraham embodies completely. His faith is not merely cognitive. It involves obedience, but the obedience is not blind; it flourishes into a knowing which is not only complete; it is a knowing that Abraham actually lives. We see Abraham's faith in his life—his embodiment, his actions, his hearing, and his interactions. Abraham's faith is his knowing. His knowing is hard-earned. It includes a full awareness of his relationship to Isaac, in all of its hope, realization, heartache, and love. It is a knowing which enters us through observation leading to communion. It is a knowing that calls to us for embodiment— some kind of enactment. The question for us becomes how, when, and in what circumstances?

LEONARDO'S VIRGIN
OF THE ROCKS

Bohm wrote in Unfolding Meaning that meaning is an aspect of reality tied to the achievement of goals and to a specific context that is so subtle and complex that it cannot be represented by any closed formula. We inhabit a universe that is imbued with profound meaning. Wholeness, love, and significance infuse and inform the universe and give it shape and form.

—**Joseph Jaworski,** *Source*

How do we become a more humanized society? How do we discover legitimate images of authentic humanity? These are questions that poet Allen Tate says are critical to society at large. Tate believes that the calling of people of letters—those who write poetry and essays—is to provide authentic images that give us insight into our ways of living and interacting with one another.

I thought of Allen Tate's writing when I recently returned to the National Gallery in London. I sat in front of Leonardo's painting, The

Virgin of the Rocks (1491–1508). It is one of the most astonishing paintings I have ever seen. The scene features the Virgin with her son the Christ child, Saint John the Baptist, and an angel. With her left hand, which is somewhat large, the Virgin blesses her Son. Her right hand supports Saint John, who is kneeling, hands clasped, in adoration of the Son of God. Saint John holds a staff which is also a cross. The legs of the Christ child are crossed, and with his right hand, he blesses Saint John. As the Christ child does so, he is supported by the angel, whose left hand gently holds his back.

The Virgin, Christ child, and Saint John form a triangle (Leonardo loved geometry). The right side of the triangle flows straight down the center of the Virgin's face to her Son. The left side flows directly from the Virgin's gaze to Saint John. The Christ child and Saint John form the points of the base of the triangle, with the Christ child slightly lower. Like with the Virgin, the gaze of the angel is on John as he worships the Christ child. The scene portrays tenderness, even as it embodies and foreshadows the deaths of the two boys, each of whom will play an essential role in the unfolding of God's involvement with the world.

The setting for this triangular portrayal of four persons is a thing of wonder, for as the title of the painting suggests, the four figures are placed among rocks. What rocks they are! The setting is cavernous; it conveys the impression that the four figures are in a dark grotto. The rocks are painted in blacks and browns in a technique called sfumato, where paint is carefully blended so that there are no distinct lines. This creates an effect of unbroken wholeness within the entire painting.

The left side of the rock formation reminds me of the jaws of a huge beast, perhaps a whale as seen from the inside, or the jaws of hell. The setting is dark and foreboding. The rocks are harsh. A child could easily be dashed, badly hurt, or even killed. At first glance, it would seem that there is nothing hospitable about the setting. It is as hard as the figures are soft, as harsh as the communion of four persons is tender. The roughness of the setting and the gentleness of the communion of persons are inversely proportional to each other. And yet, if we stay with the painting and let it settle in our imaginations, we notice that Leonardo has in fact painted flowers. Their colors seem to have more in common with the rocks, but the flowers embody a tender beauty in this harsh setting.

This raises a question: what are the four figures doing here—in this particular place? Why has Leonardo set them in this grotto of rocks? One of the important effects of this painting is to raise this very question in our imaginations. It activates our curiosity. It provokes in us a sense of wonder about the relationship between the persons of the Virgin, Saint John the Baptist, the angel, and the Christ child on the one hand and the harsh grotto-like setting on the other.

To pursue answers, there is much to notice. On the left-hand side of the painting is an opening through the jaw-like rocks that carries our gaze from the black-brown rocks to the blue-white light of sky, mountains, sea, and mist. The blues of the opening are akin to the blues in the dress of the Virgin, as the browns and grays are akin to the center opening of her dress. The dress of the Virgin and the setting of dark, cavernous rock opening to an artistic mixture of blues and whites are an inversion of each other. The flow of the garb of the angel is akin to the dress of Mary. And yet, the dress of the angel embodies more of the color of the rocks, but without a hint of the hardness that is so evident in the rocks. The relationship of colors creates a connection between two otherwise unrelated and incompatible worlds. In our imaginations, it creates the question, what do these two worlds have to do with one another? What is the nature of their relationship? Leonardo's underlying geometry once again provokes this question as we observe the rocks: there is a triangular rock formation on the upper right of the painting, through which the viewer can see blue sky. This draws our attention to the relationship between the four persons who are the primary focus of the scene and the beauty of the blue sky that we can see through the triangular opening in the rocks.

What does the scene of four persons in triangular formation portray? The two boys are assuming positions and gestures that prefigure essential roles that they will play in relationship to each other in the midst of a harsh, dangerous world. They are assuming these positions with the support and blessing of the Virgin and the angel. At the same time, the Virgin and the angel are supportively teaching the boys their roles in the life and drama that will unfold. Enfolded in this drama is deep meaning that, with the boys, it is ours to take in. The Virgin and the angel seem to understand the harsh realities that the boys, as they grow, will encounter and address. This education at the feet of the Virgin and the angel allows the boys a critical time of preparation and understanding, for the cruel realities that these boys will encounter and the manner in which they address violence suffered will ripple throughout the entire world for all time. Leonardo allows us to behold this connection in the soft blues that the clothing of Virgin and angel share with the world beyond the grotto, including the vast sky, which we the viewer can see a small portion of. The two boys, at a most tender age, are learning to anticipate something of the violence that they will face, along with their own destinies in addressing and resolving the violence. That the Christ child sits cross-legged in the lowest position of the four figures suggests that the cross, which the child embodies, serves as the base, the foundation of all that they are learning through embodiment. The cross is the instrument of cruelty on which he will die. His embodying and sitting on the cross becomes the foundation for his communion with the other three figures and the blessing that he gives. This embodiment and understanding are gently guided and supported by Virgin and angel, who play essential roles as formative teachers. Leonardo, who of course knew the roles that Saint John and the Christ child would play, portrays the preparatory embodiment of their lives in a way that draws us into this same mystery as it continues to unfold today.

My opportunity to revisit Leonardo's painting happened during the same week that Adam Lanza, age 20, horrified the world by taking a semiautomatic assault rifle and slaughtering twenty first grade children and six adults at Sandy Hook Elementary School in Connecticut. Lanza killed the 26 people after first killing his own mother, who was also owner of the guns. Lanza finally killed himself.

There have been many times when I have read stories from the first chapters of Exodus and Matthew, which we characterize by the title "The Slaughter of the Innocents." What happened at Sandy Hook Elementary School on December 14, 2012, was just that. It sickens me even to write this phrase. And yet, like the stories that Exodus and Matthew tell, Leonardo was aware of the kind of massacre to which the children of Sandy Hook were vulnerable.

Once again, the nation faces the ominous question of how to respond. Some will of course focus on gun control, some on video games, and some on mental health. It is difficult for me to imagine that a single, solitary solution will be effective. What seems clear is that the adequate protection of our children will involve a multi-lateral approach with all of us working in concert. No single person will have adequate answers, but a larger community can find answers unfolding in our active search.

In light of the horrors of the slaughter of the innocents at Sandy Hook, we have Leonardo's haunting image of the Virgin of the Rocks, which portrays two small children in the harsh setting of the cavernous grotto. It is in this place that the Virgin and angel are teaching Saint John and the Christ child to embody something of the mystery of how we become a more humanized society. With the support of the Virgin and angel, the boys are learning not only about violence and cruelty, but how to respond, to the end that violence and cruelty are transformed into blessing and peace. For what Leonardo shows us is one boy kneeling before another boy who is on the cross. As the first boy kneels in wonder and awe, he receives the blessing—the life generating spirit—of the boy of the cross. In their understanding, the two boys, with the Virgin and angel, are in communion with one another—even in the midst of a world that though harsh is still penetrated with tenderness. The boys are developing understandings that are wary of cruelty while open to tenderness. This is Leonardo's vision of humanity at its most authentic.

Thanks to him, we have this timeless image for our own reflection. It draws us into that place of deeper knowing as we seek to understand the harsh realities that we cannot escape and that it is our deepest calling to transform with the most authentic images of humanity. In other words, as we take these images into our imaginations, spend time with them, ponder, reflect, and imagine, insight begins to emerge and to unfold. Insight becomes an invaluable source for dialogue as we seek to find ways to live together with greater humanity, tenderness, peace, and creativity. In the Virgin of the Rocks, Leonardo has provided an image of great tenderness—a humanity that is in communion with one another, with learning, and with understanding. This image creates the conditions in which consciousness can be transformed.

of Sodom. Abram's encounter with the king of Sodom is interrupted by the appearance of Melchizedek. He is both king of Salem (which means peace) and high priest of God most high. Melchizedek combines both offices in one person. In other words, Melchizedek embodies the interconnection between complementary roles and functions. In the same spirit, Melchizedek brings to Abram foods of differing, but complementary qualities—bread and wine—which Melchizedek gives to Abram in celebration of the deliverance which he has successfully implemented. Bread and wine become connected with the celebration of deliverance. Abram *accepts* the bread and wine. Melchizedek blesses Abram to God. The word "blessing" refers to the life-spirit of God. The blessing, in other words, links the breath of God in Genesis 1 and 2 with the breath of Abram; it brings them together. Melchizedek then blesses God who has delivered Abram's enemies into his hands. In this blessing, Melchizedek is establishing a connection between his own breath, the breath of God, the power by which God delivered Abram's enemies into his hands, and the bread and wine which Melchizedek gives to Abram. Abram responds to Melchizedek by giving him a tithe of the property that he recovered in the battle—the very goods which Abram will refuse to accept from the king of Sodom.

What we can notice is that the encounter between Abram and Melchizedek unfolds in the midst of Abram's encounter with the king whose kingdom (Sodom) is a place of chaos and violence. The encounter is akin to what happens on the second day of creation (Genesis 1): in the midst of the primordial abyss, God creates an opening, which expands into a vast space of light and life and generativity—the heavens. What God is doing in Abram's life through Melchizedek is creating an opening—a peaceful relationship in the midst of a chaotic relationship. The relationship with Melchizedek involves connections between God's power to deliver, bread and wine, the breath of God, the breath of Abram, and Abram's reciprocal gifts to Melchizedek. These relationships and connections create an opening in the midst of a (potentially) chaotic relationship between Abram and the king of Sodom. The opening involves the priest of God Most High, who is also the king of peace. This opening makes it possible for us to recognize the connections between the power of God, bread and wine, Abram and God, and the mysterious relationship between Abram and Melchizedek.

Melchizedek appears beneath The North Rose Window of the Cathedral of Chartres. He is in the lancet window on the lower left, where he stands majestically above the diminutive Nebuchadnezzar, the king of Babylon, who destroyed the temple in Jerusalem and took the priests and the aristocracy into captivity in the early sixth century B.C. Melchizedek bears bread and wine and is the medieval picture of confidence and splendor. He is in one of five lancet windows. On the right is the high priest Aaron, brother of Moses. Just as Melchizedek went out to greet Abram on his return from deliverance, Aaron went out to meet Moses as he returned to Egypt to begin his deliverance of the Hebrew slaves. Whereas Melchizedek towers above Nebuchadnezzar, Aaron stands above Pharaoh. Melchizedek and Aaron frame King David on the inside left and King Solomon on the inside right. David carries a harp, signifying the psalms; Solomon stands for wisdom. The two great kings of Israel stand above the diminutive Saul, who is committing suicide, and Jeroboam, the mad king who is worshipping two golden calves. David and Solomon frame the center lancet window, which portrays the Virgin Mary held by her mother, Saint Anne. The Virgin and Anne are positioned directly beneath the center of the huge Rose Window, with Mary holding the Christ child. Artistically, the Rose Window portrays an unfolding from the center. This is complemented by the unfolding with St. Anne and the Virgin. What the high priests and the kings frame is the fruit of the unfolding of Mary within her mother, and above, the unfolding of the Christ child from his mother. I can't help but think of the metaphysical connection with the second and fourth days of creation in Genesis 1 (which also appear in the sculpture of the North Portal of the Cathedral). On the second day of creation, there is an expanse of the heavens, which opens and unfolds within the deep, lifeless abyss of chaos. And on the fourth day, we have the creation of expanses within the expanse of the heavens—the sun, moon, and stars. The artistic structure of the windows draws these metaphysical insights into the entire north wall. The expanses of creation are connected to the Christ child, his mother, and her mother, which are framed by the kings of psalm and wisdom, who are framed by the high priests who witness and celebrate deliverance. The windows embody the interconnections of kingship, priesthood, deliverance, bread and wine, wisdom, song, and the unfolding and expanse of creation. Metaphysically, this suggests that the justice and righteousness, which God's power of deliverance effects, are interconnected with the mysteries of creation, wisdom, psalm, and sacrament. The mysteries that the Cathedral embodies are un-severed from the everyday demands for justice, especially for those who are enslaved, oppressed, or whose freedom has been compromised.

When I stand beneath The North Rose Window, I have the feeling that it is connected to, if not calling to, the South Rose Window: the windows not only face each other, but their artistic structures are complementary inversions of one another. What they have in common are Rose Windows, with five lancets below. In the center of the South Rose Window is Christ in his glory. Directly beneath him in the center lancet is the Virgin holding the Christ child. They are flanked by four lancets—two on each side. Each lancet bears a very large prophet (from left to right, Jeremiah, Isaiah, Ezekiel, and Daniel). On the shoulders of these great prophets are four figures (Luke, Matthew, John, and Mark), who are considerably shorter. Bernard of Chartres, who was chancellor of the Cathedral from approximately 1119 to 1124, thought of scholars as dwarfs perched on the shoulders of giants (the people whom they studied). The South Wall portrays this idea artistically. The giants are the great prophets of the Old Testament. Perched on their shoulders are the four evangelists, who, owing to the insight of the four prophets, are able to see even farther than the prophets saw.

The artistic inversions of the North and South windows form a comprehensive whole, as do the stories of Abraham, when seen in concert with one another. In the North, the two great priests and two great kings trample the diminutive idolaters. In the South, the four evangelists sit on the shoulders of giant prophets who give the evangelists unqualified support. Whereas the Virgin holds the Christ child in the center of the North Rose, she stands between and among the prophets and evangelists in the South.

The windows form a complex interconnected whole. The work of the evangelists is connected not only to the work of the Virgin, the Christ child, and the prophets; it is connected to the priesthood, the monarchy, deliverance, sacrament, and the mystery of creation itself. The larger meaning of the Cathedral of Chartres is in the interconnections of wholeness. Individual sculpture and windows tell stories which are essential to the interconnected whole. This interconnected whole includes the four evangelists, whose exalted vision carries our imaginations to the heights of penetrating insight. I now want to begin to draw these essays towards concluding connections by turning to the complementary insights of the four evangelists who are perched on the shoulders of the giants of prophecy.

INSIGHT FROM MARK

Full fathom five thy father lies;
Of his bones are coral made;
Those are pearls that were his eyes:
Nothing of him that doth fade
But doth suffer a sea-change
Into something rich and strange.
—William Shakespeare, *The Tempest*

For understandable reasons, it has been difficult for many who want to follow Christ to take biblical scholarship seriously. Some who want to know the truth of the Bible and to live in intimate relationship to Christ find scholarship to trample on their sensibilities. Some responsibility for this rift may be placed on the shoulders of some (but by no means all) scholars. There are many who, noticing undeniable differences between Matthew, Mark, Luke, and John, have used those differences to try to discredit the legitimacy of the Gospels. Sadly, this has been a source of mutual frustration. People who want to know Christ as he is recognize a sense of reverence that accompanies the relationship. At the same time, biblical scholars recognize that our preconceived notions about what the Bible says are often in conflict with the actual words on the page. Anyone who reads the Bible honestly will notice conflicts of fact.

I have not, however, found the differences between the four Gospels to be discrediting. I've tried to spend ample time observing all four on their own terms. What I have discovered is that Matthew, Mark, Luke, and John all have unique insights into the meaning, mystery, manner, and consequences of the life, death, and resurrection of Jesus. I have not found the insights to be contradictory; I have found them to be complementary. And the fact that we have four Gospels of complementary insight makes us all the richer. The insights fit together much as the windows in the Cathedral. Insight is embedded in the interconnections that each writer sees. What follows will involve the first inklings of those interconnections. Together, they bring our imaginations and our bodies into a communion of knowing. Meaning unfolds in us and through us.

Mark's Gospel begins with the story of Jesus's baptism. This episode is remarkably short, and the wonder of its brevity is that it not only embodies the entire Gospel in miniature, but it also gives us the eyes to recognize insights within Mark's Gospel that we might otherwise miss. The baptism proper is a mere three sentences. Jesus goes to the Jordan, where John the Baptist immerses Jesus in the waters of the Jordan. As Jesus emerges from the waters, three things happen: the heavens split open, the spirit of God descends on Jesus in the form of a dove, and the voice of God addresses Jesus: "You are my son; with you I am well pleased." These images of the waters, the splitting open of the heavens, the descent of the dove, and the voice of God are charged with meaning.

The splitting open of the heavens is a literary apocalyptic expression. Apocalyptic literature involves the future mysteriously breaking into the present and charging the entire atmosphere of consciousness with an awareness of the future with all of its possibilities. Apocalyptic literature creates a connection between the imagination of the reader and the as yet unrealized future. The waters, on the other hand, take us back to the primordial past—the ominous deep prior to creation. In the baptism of Jesus, both the primordial past and the apocalyptic future become present in the imagination of the reader, just as they are present in Jesus. This insight is present all the way to the end of the Gospel. Just as Jesus is submerged in the waters of his baptism at the beginning, so he will be crucified and buried in the tomb at the end. And just as the heavens split open as Jesus emerges from the primordial waters, so will God, so to speak, split open the heavens, reach into the tomb, and raise his son from the dead.

The story of Jesus's baptism gives us the eyes to recognize other apocalyptic moments, or events in the Gospel. When Jesus visits the Sea of Galilee (early in the Gospel of Mark), he finds four fishermen, Peter, Andrew, James, and John, casting their nets into the sea. Jesus calls the four to leave their nets and to follow him. In the context of Mark's Gospel, why would Jesus call fishermen to follow him? Following Jesus has something to do with assisting him as he "casts his net into the sea" and draws people out who are somehow "drowning" in their own primordial abyss, and places them on solid ground. The wonder of this image in part lies in its ambiguity. Neither Jesus nor Mark defines the nature of the abyss, the deep mess in which followers of Jesus will find people who are in need of help. This critical matter depends on the willingness, insight, and judgment of the people who are willing to follow Jesus. This involves a certain amount of improvisation. We who want to follow Christ bear responsibility for recognizing and understanding people who are caught in their own chaotic abyss. Instead of limiting us, Mark's Gospel honors our imaginations. I can think of examples on the day that I compose this essay. There are significant tensions, protests, and violence in Turkey. The internal conflicts in Syria aren't anywhere close to resolution, and people are dying violent, cruel deaths daily. In the United States, there is significant unresolved conflict surrounding gun control. We aren't even close to unanimity with reference to the important question, how will we keep our children safe? Mark's Gospel makes it possible for us to recognize these serious circumstances and their connection to our responsibilities as we seek to follow Christ and to enact both his insight and power.

In the second chapter of Mark's Gospel, we encounter a story that begins with four faithful followers of Jesus carrying a man who is paralyzed. Mark doesn't name the four followers, but he does allow us to make the connection with the four fishermen whom Jesus has called at the Sea of Galilee. Jesus is at home in Capernaum. His house is packed with people who are listening to him. The four followers carrying the paralytic can't get the man through the door of Jesus's house: no one, apparently, will make room. Undaunted and undiscouraged, the four men carry the paralytic up to the roof of Jesus's house, split the roof open, and lower the paralytic until he rests at the feet of Jesus.

When I first read this story, in light of the condition of the paralytic, I would expect Jesus to heal him: *Rise, pick up your bed, and walk!* What Jesus actually does is to forgive the man's sins. This action on Jesus's part provokes serious objections. Some accuse him of blasphemy. Their accusations are not without reason: the conventional way to acquire the forgiveness of sins is to go to the temple in Jerusalem and to make the appropriate sacrifice. Jesus, without official authority, has offered forgiveness directly. This is why some accuse him of blasphemy, a capital crime. Jesus's response to this serious accusation is clever. He knows that his audience holds a cultural belief that it is not possible to be healed unless one has first been forgiven. To ratify his authority on earth to forgive sins, Jesus says to the paralytic, "Rise, pick up your bed, and go home!" The man does so. In other words, the reason behind Jesus's healing of the paralytic is to demonstrate that he has the authority to forgive sins. Jesus demonstrates his authority on terms held by those who are accusing him.

By looking at the ways in which Mark has composed his Gospel, we can easily identify the connections of this story to Mark's description of the baptism of Jesus. Just as the heavens split open when Jesus is baptized, so do his followers split open the roof of Jesus's house. Just as the Spirit of God descends on Jesus like a dove when he is baptized, so do Jesus's followers, by lowering the paralytic, cause him to descend until they lay him at the feet of Jesus. And just as the voice of God speaks to Jesus at his baptism, so does Jesus speak to the paralytic who has been laid at his feet. Just as Jesus is delivered from the primordial waters of baptism, so is the man delivered first from sin and then from the paralysis that accompanies his sin. Mark is showing us that the forgiveness and healing of the paralytic is an apocalyptic event that is connected to Jesus's baptism. The Gospel makes it possible for us to recognize this important insight.

I want to draw together some of Mark's insights by returning to an old friend—The Healing of the Woman with the Hemorrhage (5:24–34). Over the years, few stories have moved me with the depth of this story. I think this is because Mark allows us to witness and to feel both the woman's longing and the sheer humility with which she treats Jesus. For what did the woman long? She longed for delivery from both illness and exile. She had been hemorrhaging for twelve years. Twelve years of misery. Twelve years of agony. Twelve years of degradation. Twelve years of no one's having anything to do with her. Twelve years of feeling horrible on the inside. And twelve years of living on the margins. Why?

The reason is found in the fifteenth chapter of Leviticus. A woman who was hemorrhaging was regarded as unclean. As with lepers, a woman who was hemorrhaging was not allowed within the walls of the city of Jerusalem. Any *person* she touched became unclean, and every*thing* she touched became unclean as well. Consequently, the woman who was hemorrhaging was allowed contact with no one. She couldn't go to the Temple to get her sins forgiven. Instead, she lived in exile, in captivity to her illness, which was chronic, over which she had no control. The woman was not only possessed by a horrific ugliness, but she also lived in isolation. No communion. No togetherness. That was her heartbreaking plight.

To add insult and injury to injury and insult, the woman had sought help from physicians; but they had not only worsened her condition, they had taken her money in the process—all of it.

Thankfully, there was the first inkling of good news: The woman learned something about Jesus. Mark doesn't tell us *how* the woman gathered her information, nor does Mark tell us *what* she had heard. But we may assume that she heard something of what he taught, and I wouldn't be surprised if she also heard about his miracles.

Best of all, the woman found herself in a crowd that was following Jesus, pressing upon him. The woman thought to herself, "I don't need his attention. I don't need to bother him. If I could just touch him, I could be made clean."

She worked her way through the crowd to get herself to where she could reach out and just touch the hem of his garment. No sooner had she made contact than power flowed from Jesus to the woman, and she felt in her body that she was delivered from the hemorrhaging and healed of her disease.

Jesus sensed inside of himself that power had flowed from him. So he came to an abrupt stop, turned on the crowed that followed him and asked (demanded?), "Who touched me?"

When I look at the response of Jesus's disciples, I can't help but feel that they labor under an inflated sense of their own importance. The disciples were accompanying Jesus to the home of the ruler of the synagogue, who had requested of Jesus that he come and heal his twelve year old daughter. When Jesus asked, "Who touched me," the disciples objected, wanting to get on to their destination. The ruler of the synagogue would have been the most important, prestigious member of the community. Heady stuff? Did the disciples want to be seen as elites?

Jesus ignored their objections. He wanted to know who had touched him and why power had flowed out of him. I think it safe to conclude that his attention would finally have rested with the woman. She not only knew what had happened to her, but she also understood what she had (perhaps unintentionally) done: she has approached (sneaked up behind?) Jesus, touched him, taken his healing power without having first asked for it, and so doing, she has made him unclean, forcing him to bear her sickness on himself.

Mark tells us that the woman came forward in fear and trembling, bowed before Jesus with her face to the ground, and told Jesus the whole truth. And what was the whole truth? Years of suffering. Years of agony. Years of exile and isolation. The degrading treatment of the physicians. Hearing about Jesus. The glimmer of hope. How she had found herself in this crowd that was pressing upon him. How she had reasoned with herself: I don't need his attention. If I could just touch him. How she desperately tried to reach him. How she just got hold of the hem of his garment. How the power had flowed into her. How she had felt the God-given blessing of relief! *O, the relief!* And then, how Jesus stopped, turned, and demanded, "Who touched me?" Mark says that the woman told Jesus the whole truth—everything.

By custom, Jesus has the right to be furious with the woman. She has taken his healing power without first asking permission, and so doing, has made Jesus unclean. Anger, however, has no place in his thinking. Instead, Jesus addresses the woman as a member of his family: he calls her "Daughter." "Daughter, your faith has made you well. Go in peace, and be healed of your disease."

I want to observe something of the ways in which the perspectives and actions of the woman, Jesus, and Mark as Gospel writer all come together. At the end of this story, when Jesus addresses the woman as his daughter, he tells the woman that her faith has made her well. What does Jesus mean by this? We find the answer not in a belief system that the woman articulates, but in her action. The woman's faith is that she can be connected to Jesus. And when she reaches out and touches him, enacting her faith, she establishes the reality of the connection. The woman's faith is that she can touch Jesus, and he will heal her. It is that simple, that straightforward—a connection. Her faith is that she belongs to Christ. Her faith is that she can be in communion with Jesus. The woman may not yet have a secondary version of faith that she can articulate or write an essay on, but this does not detract from a faith that is primary—completely substantive. The woman has a faith that she has enacted. So doing, she has learned that she is a member of Christ's family. She is completely connected. She belongs.

What about the actions to which the woman is connected— the actions of Jesus. In addressing the woman as "Daughter," Jesus is both establishing her as a member of his own family—his own communion—and calling to our attention that this, too, is an apocalyptic moment, an apocalyptic event. At the beginning of Mark's Gospel—the baptism of Jesus—when we hear the voice of God, it addresses Jesus as God's son. The first time in the Bible that God addresses someone as his son is in the fourth chapter of Exodus at the conclusion of God's call on Moses to demand of Pharaoh the liberation of the Hebrew slaves. God directs Moses to tell Pharaoh, "Israel is my firstborn son." What God wants for his firstborn son is deliverance from slavery and oppression. The sons and daughters of God are the people whom God is delivering. At Jesus's baptism, when God addresses Jesus as his son, he is disclosing that he will deliver Jesus from the tomb by raising him from the dead. The sons and daughters of God are the ones whom God is delivering by transforming them into members of God's family. By addressing the woman as daughter, Jesus is connecting her both to his baptism and to God's power to deliver her. The power by which God is delivering her from her illness and returning her from the exile of uncleanness to full membership in the family of God is the same power by which God delivered the Hebrews from slavery in Egypt and the same power by which God will raise Jesus from the dead. These events form an interconnection of both primordial and apocalyptic import.

The action by which Jesus achieves this outcome is remarkable. His action bears almost identical resemblance to what he does in the last supper in Mark 14. When Jesus celebrates the supper with his disciples, he takes bread, blesses the bread, breaks it, and gives it to his disciples with the words, "Take, this is my body, given for you." Jesus does something similar with the wine. After the supper, Jesus goes to the Garden of Gethsemane with three of his disciples. It is while he is in the garden that people come to arrest Jesus. His response and actions are completely premeditated. Jesus neither fights nor flees. Instead, he presents himself to his captors. So doing, Jesus transforms his own being taken into a gift: he gives himself to the people who are taking him.

It is by no means difficult to see the connection between what Jesus does with the bread and wine in the supper and the action he takes when he is taken. Just as Jesus, in the supper, presents broken bread to his disciples with the words, "Take, this is my body given for you," so also he transforms his own being taken into a gift in the garden. This is the great transformation. What Jesus delivers at the supper bears a connection to what he enacts, what he actually does with his own body as he is taken for mock trial and crucifixion. Both the supper and Jesus's actions are connected to the Passover and to the bread and wine that Melchizedek presents to Abram as he returns from delivering Lot and the people of Sodom. Jesus renders the actions of deliverance with the greatest of possible clarity.

Jesus's interaction with the woman with the hemorrhage bears this same transformation. The woman took his healing power without Jesus's consent. Instead of reacting in anger, Jesus addresses her as a member of his family. So doing, Jesus transforms her act of taking into an act of receiving. His power becomes her gift, even as his words establish her membership in the communion of those whom God is delivering. The embodied enactment of the sacramental words, "Take, this is my body given for you," delivers people from captivity, alienation, isolation, and exile into the communion of fellowship and love. This is the reason for our existence. Jesus's actions in the most difficult, demanding, and challenging of situations transform seemingly impossible circumstances into the possibility for interconnected wholeness. His actions are primary, and they create the capacity for the communion of fully knowing primary relationships.

As Mark brings this understanding to awareness in both our imaginations and our bodies, he also shows us that Jesus's involvement with the woman with the hemorrhage is of apocalyptic import. Framing the story of The Woman with the Hemorrhage is the story of The Healing of the Daughter of the Ruler of the Synagogue. Jairus approaches Jesus because Jairus's twelve year old daughter is sick unto death. Jesus consents to go to her aid. It is while walking to the home of the ruler of the synagogue that Jesus has his encounter with the woman who has been hemorrhaging for twelve years. The genius of Mark's literary insight shows us that the solution to the kinds of challenges and problems posed by the critical illness of the daughter of the ruler of the synagogue are addressed and resolved in the story in the middle, for it is after dealing with the woman with the hemorrhage that Jesus completes his journey to Jairus's home, where he speaks the words, *Talitha cumi*: "I say to you, little girl, arise."

We have already seen the one connection between the stories of Jesus's baptism and the woman with the hemorrhage, where the words of God to Jesus, "You are my son," are connected to Jesus's words to the woman, "Daughter, your faith has made you well." Mark's literary composition shows us an additional essential connection. Just as the heavens, at Jesus's baptism, split open, disclosing the baptism as an apocalyptic moment, with the future mysteriously breaking into the present for deliverance, so does the story of The Woman with the Hemorrhage split the story of The Healing of the Daughter of the Ruler of the Synagogue in two. The Healing of the Woman with the Hemorrhage embodies the breaking in of the same reality with which Jesus addresses the horrific circumstances of his arrest for trial and crucifixion with the bread and wine of his last supper—the transformation that capacitates us for interconnections that create the possibility for communion, wholeness, and peace.

INSIGHT FROM LUKE

This is a strange repose, to be asleep
With eyes wide open; standing, speaking, moving,
And yet so fast asleep.
—William Shakespeare, *The Tempest*

At a meal in Emmaus, the disciples have their eyes opened. They are able to recognize the presence of the risen Christ with them. The opening of their eyes involves a long process. It isn't instantaneous. It is, however, fascinating.

Earlier on that day, the women had discovered the empty tomb. It was dawn. A group of women, three of whom Luke names, carried spices to the tomb. When they arrived, the women discovered that the stone had been rolled away from the entrance to the tomb. When they entered the tomb, they did not find the body of Jesus. Instead, they found two men (*duo andrés*) in dazzling apparel. The two men ask the women why they seek the living among the dead. The body of Christ is not in the tomb because he has risen from the dead. The two men then remind the women of truths which everyone is struggling to bear in mind: *that the*

Son of man must be delivered into the hands of sinful men and be crucified and on the third day rise. It is at this point that the women remember the words that Jesus had spoken to them and return to the eleven disciples to share with them what they have experienced and known.

The issue of reminding his followers of the necessity—the essentiality—of Jesus's suffering, death, and resurrection, will recur on the road to Emmaus. It is difficult for the disciples to keep matters of mystery clearly in mind. Under pressure and duress, it is also difficult for them to keep clear minds. Sustaining clear-headedness is challenging at best. It is not, however, impossible. As the women are reminded, they remember his words. This is one of the keys to entering and re-entering the mysterious world of primary knowing: remembering.

Later that same day, two disciples are making the seven mile journey to Emmaus. One of the disciples is named Cleopas. Luke does not tell us the name of the other disciple. As they walk, the two men discuss the events that have unfolded. The risen Christ draws near, begins to listen in to their conversation and to ask them what they are talking about. The two men stand still. They appear to be stunned by the question. They can't believe that there is someone who is unaware of what Jesus has been through and what they, in response, are going through. The two disciples come to an abrupt stop and ask if he is the only person in all of Israel who doesn't know about the things that have unfolded.

The risen Christ asks them, "What things?"

The two disciples begin to review what has happened. They give a fairly detailed description. They talk about Jesus as a prophet. They talk about his mighty words and deeds. They talk about the chief priests and scribes delivering Jesus up to death—condemning Jesus and crucifying him. And then, they talk about their incredulity over the report of the women who went to the tomb and returned claiming to have seen a vision of angels along with the absence of Jesus's body.

They talk about their disappointments. The disciples had hoped that Jesus was the one who would redeem Israel. The impression that they give is that they expected Jesus to impose redemption on the people—from above, or from without. But what Jesus actually does is to join those captives who are in need of redemption and then to lead them out of captivity—much as Virgil and Beatrice did for Dante. This is what Jesus actually does with Cleopas and the unnamed disciple. They are captive to their grief. They are paralyzed; they are on the edge of despair. Their expectations have been shattered. They are heartbroken, and the risen Christ joins them right where they are. When he speaks, it is with a kind question. The question allows them to observe the events that have been unfolding by describing them. Their description includes what they *thought* was going to happen— what they expected, or anticipated—and then how things took a turn and went in a different, unexpected direction. He was crucified: condemned by the chief priests and rulers, and crucified. That was the first, devastating turn of events. In every respect, it was cause for overwhelming, debilitating, consuming, paralyzing despair. It was the end of hope. Nothing could have been worse.

This was followed by another unexpected turn of events: that very morning, some women reported going to the tomb and finding it empty, seeing a vision of angels who said that Jesus was alive. This was completely amazing, but they didn't know what to make of it. Some in their group went to the tomb, which was as the women had reported, but they did not see Jesus.

Jesus then responds to what they have reported. He does not call attention to himself; they do not yet know that it is he. He first raises another question: this is in direct response to what they have described. He asks, was it not necessary—needful, right, fitting, or proper—for the Christ to suffer and enter into his glory? What Jesus is asking is if the suffering, crucifixion, and resurrection of Christ were not, in some irreducible sense, essential. The risen Christ then interprets, from the scriptures, all matters necessary to understanding what has unfolded and what is still unfolding right before their eyes.

What Luke does not do is to describe or report the content of Jesus's interpretation. We know the result, or the outcome of his teaching: their hearts burned. Jesus's words enkindled a flame that affected their consciousness. We do not know if it was a seed of fire, a slow-burning ember, or if the flame spread like wildfire throughout the vast regions of imagination. We do know that in some self-evident, compelling sense, Jesus's words of interpretation set them on fire.

Without the actual contents of Jesus's interpretation, what are we to make of what Jesus is actually doing? How do we proceed? We have Jesus's question: was it not necessary? Were these events somehow unnecessary? Were they a misfit? Were they improper? Unessential? Did the events fail, somehow, to work?

We do know that they were connected to Moses and the prophets. The question is how? What is the relationship between the events involving Jesus that unfolded and what we read in our scripture? In what sense are the death and resurrection of Jesus essential?

Before we search out connections, it is important to pause and consider the effect of Luke's Gospel. The story itself draws in our imaginations, ignites them, and sends them on a quest to find answers to Jesus's question. What begins as a question addressed to Cleopas and the unnamed disciple becomes a question that the risen Christ addresses to us. Because Luke does not give the answer to Jesus's questions directly, *it becomes our responsibility to discover connections.* This gives us the opportunity to search the Old Testament and to discover how the mysteries it embodies are connected to Jesus. As we do so, the risen Christ creates a small opening in the abyss of confusion in our imaginations. As the opening expands, our eyes are opened. What is there for us to discover? What can we begin to see?

As we read for the first time, we become observers, overseeing Jesus in conversation with disciples whose understanding is held in a kind of captivity, held from recognizing and knowing the risen Lord. We are observers as Jesus asks them questions that lead them to recall, to remember, to observe what is in the files of their memory. We observe the two disciples as they begin to piece things together. We observe as Jesus's questions lead to the first inklings of understanding.

Then the story takes a turn that directly affects our involvement in the story. The risen Christ asks a question that they cannot answer and that he will answer for them. It is a long answer. It is a substantive answer. It is an answer that involves the broadest understanding of the Old Testament. Jesus's answer to the question he himself poses is comprehensive, thorough, and mesmerizing. The disciples are completely captivated by the answer to the question that Jesus gives. Jesus's answer moves them steadily into a full, rich understanding of their deepest questions. They find Jesus's answers to be completely satisfying. The question is the same question that the two men in dazzling apparel asked the women at the tomb: "Was it not necessary that the Son of Man suffer these things and enter into his glory?" And then, beginning with Moses and the prophets, the risen Christ opens their minds to understanding.

Here's where the effect of the story takes a sharp turn for us as we read and seek to understand—to sort out the pieces of the mystery and to assimilate them in the tapestry of our imaginations: Luke doesn't tell us the contents of what Jesus teaches them. There isn't a word. It's as though he assumes that we already know the answer. And if we will be honest with ourselves—especially in those first couple of readings—we will realize the embarrassing truth that we still have lots to learn. This is especially true for people who "have it all figured out," as though the gospel and faith in Christ can be reduced to a tidy formula or theory—like a theory of salvation or a formula for atonement. The problem is that Christ isn't a theory or a formula, any more than any other living person is a theory or a formula. The problem with formulae is that once you come up with a formula about God, the formula becomes the thing and you can dispense with God. This is why Job will not settle for his friends' theories about why he is suffering: he knows that the theories about suffering and the formulae about God are not only unsatisfactory; they are no substitute for knowing God and interacting with God directly.

So what does Luke do by telling us that Jesus, in answer to his own question, gives the most mesmerizing, satisfying answer to the question, but without telling us one word about what Jesus says? Luke is drawing us in, provoking and mobilizing our own imaginations fueled by curiosity to participate in the active search for answers with which we resonate—answers that are true because they are self-evident. What Luke is doing is to transform us from passive recipients into active curious investigators of the Old Testament who recognize the essential connections between the reality of mystery embodied in Moses and the prophets with the reality of mystery that is unfolding in their lives and ours—in which we play essential roles.

How, then, are the suffering, death, and resurrection of Jesus connected to the Old Testament? What can *we* observe? What do the suffering, death, and resurrection of Jesus have to do with necessity? In what sense are these realities essential?

There is plenty for us to observe, especially if we are willing to take the long view. I think it important to begin with Genesis 1 because this story portrays the metaphysical formatting of the cosmos. It involves the creation of a world that embodies generativity that established a field in which life and creativity can unfold. In the broadest of terms, when God created the heavens and the earth, he delivered the abyss from *chaos* to give birth to a whole new *world*. The world is a cosmos: it has direction, moving from alpha to omega, beginning to completion. God's creative imagination, insight, and power drive everything that God accomplishes from Genesis 1 through Revelation 22. With this same creativity, God delivered the Hebrews from the *chaos* of slavery in Egypt to the *world* of the promise land, which God intended as its own cosmos of creativity that would embody justice and love. With this same creative power, God delivered the Jews from the *chaos* of captivity in Babylon to return to the *world* of their own homeland. This is the same reality that we witness in Luke 24: what the disciples—the followers of Jesus—are witnessing is Jesus as he is delivered from the *chaos* of captivity and death to life in communion with the *world* by means of the resurrection from the dead. This unfolds at early dawn, which also connects this day to the first day of creation in Genesis 1.

Still, why was it necessary that Jesus suffer? Why was it necessary for Jesus to be delivered into the hands of sinful men and be crucified and on the third day rise? Jesus refused to lord it over others. In Luke's Gospel, Jesus emphasizes this in concert with his last supper (Luke 22:24–27). By allowing himself to be arrested, Jesus is placing himself in a position not unlike the Hebrews who were enslaved in Egypt, or not unlike the Jews who were taken into captivity in Babylon. By refusing to lord it over others, suffering betrayal and denial, transforming his own being taken by the Romans into a gift (*Take, this is my body given to you*), Jesus connects himself—his own essential self—to the places in history where God led his people from captivity and unspeakable atrocities, transforming them into a new creation. Moreover, what the risen Christ is doing—right here in Luke's Gospel—is to join two of his disciples as they are held captive to debilitating grief, as they are held hostage to their own unwillingness to remember, to reflect, to search for vital answers, and to understand. The risen Christ joins them where they are paralyzed and shattered, where their own creative capacities for understanding have been incarcerated, and slowly, with patient deliberation, leads them from ignorance to understanding, blindness to sight, darkness to light.

This sense of actually joining people in their captivity and leading them to freedom and wholeness and communion is embodied in the seventh chapter of Luke, one of several of Luke's stories that are deeply moving. This particular story, among other matters of import, shows a stark contrast between a woman who becomes connected to Jesus in a way that is so profound that it gives birth to deep gratitude, and Simon the Pharisee, whose invitation to Jesus has nothing to do with hospitality, but is a smokescreen for his own desire to take Jesus into captivity through entrapment.

The duties of host to guest were sacred—not only in Judaism, but throughout the entire Middle East, stretching all the way to India. Simon has invited Jesus to his home for dinner. When a guest entered the home of the host, the host would customarily greet the guest with a kiss. The servants would then come in and wash the guest's feet. If the host couldn't afford servants, he would wash his guest's feet himself. After the foot-washing, the host would then anoint the guest with oil, which had a fragrance, like perfume. These were the customs incumbent on the host during the time of Jesus. They were the host's way of telling the guest, "You are welcome here."

Simon was doubly obligated to offer these common courtesies to Jesus: Simon had actually *invited* Jesus to dinner. Simon's treatment of Jesus wasn't close to being hospitable. That is because his motive for inviting Jesus to the party had nothing to do with hospitality. Simon was bent on entrapping and discrediting Jesus as a pretext for incarceration. At the very least, Simon wanted to damage Jesus's reputation and turn people against him. He treated Jesus like an unwelcome guest.

Luke tells us that they *reclined* for the meal. This means that they lay on their sides on sofas, propping themselves up on the left elbow. The meal began when the servants would bring a large bowl of food and place the food in the center of the table. With their right hands, the guests would reach into the common bowl and take the food.

As they are sharing the meal, a woman enters Simon's home. She kneels behind Jesus, where he is reclining. The woman weeps over Jesus's feet, covers his feet with her tears, and dries the tears with her hair. The woman then smothers his feet with kisses. The Greek word that Luke uses is *kataphiléo*. It means to kiss *passionately*. The woman then takes oil, which is in her possession, and rubs the oil onto Jesus's feet.

Simon is scandalized. He recognizes the woman as a prostitute. The clues are clear, especially when we consider the social position of women in the time of Jesus. A woman had no rights. She had no economic or political power. Nor was a woman allowed possessions. The only thing a woman "owned" was her dowry, which was never exclusively in her possession because she exercised no power over it. Typically, the person who controlled her dowry was her father, and he customarily gave the dowry to her husband when he gave his daughter to be married. A woman was not allowed to speak to a man in public. And if she did, she brought so much disgrace upon her husband that he had the right to divorce her: all he had to do was to put her shoes outside, and according to custom, she was compelled to leave. Having no social standing, a woman had no opportunity for legitimate employment. This left the divorced woman with a tragic choice—prostitution or starvation.

There are other clues that tell us that the woman in this story is a prostitute. Culturally respectable women wore their hair in a bun. Prostitutes wore their hair down to lure men. This woman used her hair to dry Jesus's feet. Luke also tells us that the woman had oil—likely a tool of her trade—with which she anointed Jesus's feet.

A final clue to the woman's social standing is her behavior. Respectable women didn't crash dinner parties, and they didn't behave as this woman is behaving.

To understand the force of the circumstance that Luke's story portrays, it is important to remember that according to Leviticus, people who have recently had intimate relations are ceremonially unclean. Anyone or anything they touch also becomes unclean. A prostitute would be perpetually unclean. When she touches Jesus, he becomes unclean. The sofa on which he reclines becomes unclean, and if Jesus then touches the common bowl from which the entire party is eating, the food becomes unclean as well. This would completely spoil Simon's dinner party.

None of this is lost on Simon: he is a Pharisee, a *learned* man. Simon seems, however, less concerned with the spoiling of the dinner party, but completely bent on discrediting Jesus. This is because Simon's motive is entrapment. Luke tells us this by communicating Simon's thoughts: "If this man were a real prophet, he would know who and what sort of woman this is who is touching him, for she is a sinner."

Jesus responds to Simon directly: "I have something to say to you."

"Speak on, Teacher."

Jesus responds with a parable: "A certain creditor has two debtors. Both owed him money. The first one owed him five hundred day's wages, and the other owed fifty. Neither could repay the creditor, so he forgave both of their debts. Now here's the question: Which debtor would love the creditor more?"

Simon's answers, "The one who was forgiven more."

Jesus responds, "You have answered correctly. Do you see this woman? When I entered your house, you gave me no water for my feet, but she has wet my feet with her tears and wiped them with her hair. You gave me no kiss, but she has not stopped covering my feet with kisses. You did not anoint my head with oil, but she has anointed my feet with ointment."

Jesus then drives home the truth: "Therefore, I tell you, her sins, which were many, have been forgiven. This is why she has shown great love." Her gratitude is proof that she has *received* forgiveness. Gratitude has given birth to love.

In responding to Simon's challenge, Jesus doesn't deny the magnitude of the sins that the woman has committed. Her sin is like five hundred day's wages. Her sin, in other words, was great. What Jesus emphasizes is the larger story of what has happened in the life of the woman and what her response to Jesus embodies. The woman encountered Jesus. She found that Jesus cared about her as a person. He treated the woman with dignity and respect. Jesus recognized her as human, and he responded to her humanity. He welcomed her with the honor befitting a child of God. When Jesus looked at the woman, he may or may not have seen a prostitute. What is certain is that he saw a child of God. First and last, a child of God merits honor. She merits the deepest of love and respect, and one of the greatest responses of deep love and respect is forgiveness. This is what Jesus had offered the woman. Jesus joined the woman by connecting with her humanity. He conveyed understanding for the tragic choice between prostitution and starvation. By offering her the forgiveness of sin, he led the woman from captivity to sin into the wholeness of communion in great love. The woman's spontaneous response was gratitude. The deepest humanity of the woman called to the deepest love in Jesus. This is what we see unfold in the home of Simon the Pharisee, even as Simon is treating Jesus with hostility and contempt.

For Jesus to deliver the woman from her own captivity, it was essential that he somehow join her in her captivity by responding to her humanity. In this way, his forgiving her established the vital connectivity in which he could lead her out of captivity into the communion of wholeness. In the home of Simon the Pharisee, whereas communion should have unfolded in the dinner party itself, it actually unfolded in the whole world constituted by the woman who anoints Jesus. This communion of wholeness is captured artistically on one of the most moving stained glass windows of the Cathedral of Chartres: the Mary Magdalene Window. In the Middle Ages, tradition thought her to be the woman who washed Jesus's feet and anointed him. In the window, the guests don't recline, but sit at table. The woman occupies the lowest position, from which she leans, under the table, towards Jesus's feet, which she enfolds with luxurious hair. The alabaster flask of oil rests on the frame of the window, slightly tilted towards Jesus. The artists who designed the window have captured her love born of gratitude, born of forgiveness.

Another story from Luke that is embodied in stained glass in the Cathedral is The Parable of the Prodigal son, perhaps the best known, most beloved parable in all of Scripture. I want to draw this essay on Luke's insight to a conclusion by commenting on the father in this parable. It was not possible for the father to join the younger son in his self-inflicted captivity to avarice, gluttony, and lust. When the younger son asked for his share of his father's property, the boy essentially ran away from home. But when, having restored a sense of his own sanity, the boy returned home, the father could join the elder son in his self-imposed exile of envy. By actually joining—connecting with—his elder son, the father positioned himself to advocate and plead for the restoration of the interconnections of the family. The father's actions would have been both different and significantly less compelling had he simply stood at the door of his home and called to the elder son to come in. Jesus does not tell us how the elder son actually responded. But he does show us the father creating the optimum possibility for the re-enkindling of communion as he actually joins the elder son in his self-inflicted captivity.

The action of Jesus with the woman and the father with the elder son show us something of the necessity of the suffering of Jesus. He finds it essential actually to join us in exile, to connect with us in our captivity, to the end that deliverance and restoration might be effective, that they might create the possibility for interconnections leading to communion—in a word, wholeness.

In the story of Jesus joining Cleopas and the unnamed disciple on the road to Emmaus, Luke makes it possible for us to understand *something* of the necessity of this suffering. For Christ to deliver people from captivity, it is essential that he join them in the circumstances that hold them hostage. Only with that vital connection secure can he then lead us from captivity to freedom in love.

Christ found it essential to join his own disciples in their own captivity to both grief and ignorance. Christ was willing to play this essential role to its fullness. This in turn drew Cleopas and the unnamed disciple into their essential roles of learning to recognize Jesus, whom they could then assist as he seeks to open the eyes of others. As they arrive at Emmaus, Jesus appears to be going farther. They urge Jesus to remain with them. Jesus consents. They gather in a room for a meal.

And, of course, the risen Christ takes bread, blesses the bread, breaks the bread, and gives it to his disciples. It is then that their eyes are opened. It is then that they recognize that it is he—that he is right there with them. And it is at this moment that he can absent himself.

Why is it this particular moment? In this moment, they have made all of the essential connections. They could not have accomplished this without his presence. In his presence, they have done so. The connections are complete. The disciples can now see. Their knowing is primary.

It can be so with us as well. Luke creates this possibility, as does the Cathedral.

INSIGHT FROM JOHN

Stockdale was a supremely private man and seldom chose to talk of his faith or the Divine. However, he said that during his confinement, at the moment of maximum danger to his life, suddenly the face of Christ "popped out of nowhere" in front of him—the same face, he said, he saw every Sunday on the big stained-glass window of the U.S. Naval Academy chapel just behind the altar. "He's looking right into me, just like he used to when I was a plebe sitting before Him at mandatory chapel every Sunday, praying that I could make it at Annapolis." At the very same moment of the vision, he was able to make split-second decisions that enabled him to avoid detection of his secret messages by two guards who had just entered his cell.

—**Joseph Jaworski,** *Source*

One of the mysteries in the Gospel of John has to do with Jesus's appearance to Mary when she visits the tomb, an episode that is included in The Mary Magdalene Window in the Cathedral of Chartres. When Mary finally recognizes Jesus and reaches out to him, he says, "Do not hold me, for I have not yet ascended to the father." Why does Jesus say this to her? What does he mean?

We don't *at first* know the answer to this question (at least, I don't!), but it is the kind of mystery that, like with Jesus's conversation with two disciples on the road to Emmaus, piques our curiosity and activates our imaginations. To understand this cryptic response, it is important to know something of the larger context of the story of the resurrection in the Gospel of John.

When it comes to reading the Bible, I think the biggest eye-opener for me was becoming aware of the multitude and significance of interconnections. This is especially true of the Gospel of John. At the beginning of his Gospel, John lays out mysteries that come to fruition at the end of his Gospel. John tells us that all of creation comes to completion in the resurrection of Jesus. What John describes in the prologue in the first chapter comes to fulfillment in his story of the resurrection in the twentieth. What kinds of mysteries does John write about?

The light shines in the darkness, and the darkness
has not comprehended the light.
That which comes to being in him is life,
and the life is the light of all people.
He came to his own home, and his own people did not recognize him.
The word became flesh and dwelt among us full of grace and truth.
We have beheld his glory, full of grace and truth.

Then we come to our first encounter with John the Baptist. John always points people to Jesus: "Behold the Lamb of God who takes away the sin of the world!" John points to Jesus directly. He wants people to *encounter* Jesus—to see for themselves. John wants people in possession of their own knowing.

This is followed by Jesus's first encounter with people. They want to know "where he is staying," and Jesus tells them to "come and see." John's Gospel is always interested in people's direct involvement with Jesus. This is what leads to understanding. It is essential that our involvement be primary if he is to deliver us—to move us from darkness to light. As we read the Gospel of John, we become witnesses as people make the journey from ignorance to understanding. This makes it possible for us to join them in the journey.

When Mary Magdalene goes to the tomb (John 20:1), it is still dark. She sees that the tomb is empty, but she does not yet understand that Jesus has risen from the dead. *The light shines in the darkness, but the darkness does not comprehend the light;* Mary does not yet understand: she is "in the dark." The risen Christ appears to Mary, and the risen Christ later appears to his disciples: *The word became flesh and dwelt among us full of grace and truth.* When Mary first sees the risen Christ, she doesn't recognize him; she thinks he is the gardener: *He came to his own home, and his own people did not recognize him.* The risen Christ shows them his wounds: *We have beheld his glory, full of grace and truth.* The risen Christ breathes on them and says, "Receive the Holy Spirit": *That which comes to being in him is life, and the life is the light of all people.* All of the mysteries that John lays out in the beginning of the Gospel come to fruition in the resurrection.

When the disciples who witnessed the risen Christ tell Thomas, he refuses to believe until he witnesses the wounds for himself. Thomas wants to *behold the Lamb of God;* he wants to *come and see—* to see for himself.

Taking an even longer view, we see that what unfolds in the Gospel of John, especially the resurrection, brings the first chapters of Genesis to fulfillment as well. John begins with an echo of Genesis 1 when he writes, "In the beginning was the word." And just as the wind, or breath of God was blowing over the deep, and just as God breathed into Adam's nostrils and he became a living person, so does the risen

Christ breathe on his disciples. In John's Gospel, we are witnesses as creation comes to fulfillment.

By centering his Gospel in creation, John shows us something of the composition of the world—how it is formatted, how the world is put together. The formatting involves connections, including the relationship between words, beliefs, and action. The words involve hearing and knowing. I use the verb "knowing" as opposed to the noun "knowledge" because hearing and knowing are active and involved—fully engaged. When we hear the words that Jesus speaks—when we drink them in, treasure them, seek to understand them—the consequence is that he knows us. This is a wonderfully mysterious paradox: in John's Gospel, when we provide hospitality for Christ's words, he knows us in our hospitality. The first time the Bible shows us this kind of hospitality is with Abraham in Genesis 18. Abraham offered the most exquisite of hospitality to three men. In the words of the Epistle to the Hebrews, Abraham found himself to be entertaining angels unaware. John will later show us this same reality in chapter 13 as Jesus washes his disciples' feet. To the degree that people treasure both the words and the works of Jesus, he knows them.

In John's Gospel, these are the people to whom he gives eternal life. We later learn that eternal life is the knowing that the Father and the son have for one another: It is active, receptive, and expresses unconditional value—one for the other and both for the relationship.

This also involves a certain protection. Christ's claim is that when he knows us, no one will snatch us from his hand. He gives reasons: *when we treasure the words that Christ speaks and embodies, Christ knows us.* When he knows us, we are members of the communion of the Father and the Son. This membership is the mystery of delectation—to be explored, understood, and enjoyed—actively, quietly, without fanfare, with full, unfolding awareness.

Another occasion when Jesus evokes paradoxical mystery is when he washes his disciples' feet. At a critical moment, Jesus says, "Where

I am going, you cannot come." This is another of those phrases in the Gospel. It both complements Jesus's statement to Mary, "Do not hold me, for I have not yet ascended to the father," and like that statement, provokes curiosity and activates our imaginations, moving us to explore the "many rooms" of the Gospel itself. As Jesus washes his disciples' feet, he does so in the midst of betrayal and denial: "During supper, when the devil had already put it into the heart of Judas Iscariot, Simon's son, to betray him," Jesus washes his disciples' feet. Then, after the story of the foot-washing, Jesus tells his disciples, "One of you will betray me." Denial (Peter) and betrayal (Judas) make for an abyss of horrific chaos and dread. The very people whom Jesus is closest to—the ones on whom he *should* be able to count—deny and betray him. This is beyond awful.

It is in the midst of the horror of being betrayed and denied that Jesus washes his disciples' feet. This is a wonder-filled act of cleansing, containing strong echoes of Jesus's first miracle/sign—turning the water into wine (John 2). At the wedding at Cana, there were six stone jars that were used for cleansing—the Jewish rites of purification. Jesus directed that the jars be filled with water. Here in chapter 13, John's Gospel brings cleansing to fulfillment as we become witnesses to Jesus as he washes his disciples' feet. Drawn *into* the story, *we* become cleansed.

This act of cleansing in the midst of an abyss of denial and betrayal draws us back again to Genesis 1. In the beginning was a dark, formless abyss. The breath of God blows over the face of the deep. God says, "Let there be light." On the second day, God creates a small opening in the midst of the abyss, and the opening becomes an expanse of light, life, and generativity. The expanse is called the heavens, and the heavens begin as a small opening in the midst of an abyss of chaos. When Jesus washes his disciples' feet, he creates an opening, which becomes an expanse within the chaotic abyss of denial and betrayal. This expanse creates an opening in our own imaginations. We ourselves are cleansed and purified—right in the midst of our own denial and betrayal.

As Jesus interprets this experience for his disciples, he says, "Now the Son of Man has been glorified, and God has been glorified in him." Jesus goes on to say, "If God has been glorified in him [Jesus], God shall also glorify Jesus in himself." John's insight here is nothing short of remarkable: he recognizes that there is a mysterious sense in which God and Christ are enfolded into one another. This embodies the reality conveyed in Genesis 1 in the fourth day of creation. Just as God creates an expanse of light and life within the abyss on Day 2, God creates expanses of light and life within the expanse of the heavens on Day 4. On Day 4, we have expanses within the expanse—life unfolding in life, light unfolding in light. In John 13, he tells us that God is glorified in Christ. The paradox is that God shall also glorify Christ in God himself.

We can spell out John's insight explicitly: by washing his disciples' feet, Jesus glorified God inside of himself. Jesus then completed his enactment of love as he laid down his life for his friends. In response to Christ's laying down his life for his friends, God glorified Christ in himself. When Jesus washed his disciples' feet, he completed the rite of purification represented by the six stone jars (which are echoes of the six days on which God created the heavens and the earth). When Jesus then laid down his life for his friends, God served new wine from the jars of purification.

We can put this still another way: the six stone jars of purification and Jesus washing his disciples' feet, cleansing and purifying them, come to fulfillment as Jesus is crucified on the cross. By laying down his life for his friends, *Jesus enfolded God into himself.* God responded to his only begotten son's laying down his life for his friends by *enfolding Jesus into himself—raising Jesus from the dead, transforming the water of cleansing and purification into the wine of fellowship, communion, and love.*

This is why Mary, when she first encounters the risen Christ, cannot yet hold him. The resurrection of Jesus from the dead becomes complete when God finally enfolds his risen son into himself. So doing,

God and Christ become mysteriously enfolded into one another. Their relationship becomes complete, the interconnections whole. That is when we are to reach out and touch them—as a matter of imagination wed to will. We become whole as we enfold the interconnections of the Father and the Son into ourselves. This is the Great Mystery.

There are occasions in the Gospel of John when Jesus emphasizes that he is going away—that it is *essential* that he go away. It is when Jesus returns to the Father that their relationship becomes complete. In love, the Father is enfolded into the Son, and the Son is enfolded into the father. The relationship between the Father and the Son can then be enfolded into us in our faith. As our faith comes to fruition, it comes to have content. The content is the mystery of relationship between the Father and the Son mysteriously enfolded in one another. This relationship lies at the heart of their essence. Because their relationship is complete, their world is complete.

This is the mystery that we encounter as we come to know Christ as he is. In loving him, we treasure his words. As we treasure his words, they become enfolded into our imaginations. The words themselves embody the relationship between the Father and the Son. His words enfold their relationship into our imaginations. As the relationship between God and Christ is enfolded in our imaginations, our knowing becomes primary.

At best, it is a challenge for us to bear these words. The reason is straightforward. Whereas the relationship between the Father and the Son is complete—eternal—we are incomplete. We are still emerging and unfolding. To cite Flannery O'Connor, the goodness in us is still under construction. Embracing the words of the Father and the Son and the reality that their words embody is difficult because whereas their relationship is complete, we are incomplete. Their relationship is eternal, and we are still emerging. This is the great paradox: through love and faith, the complete is enfolded into the incomplete: the relationship between God and Christ makes its home in us.

Recognizing the difficulty that we who are incomplete have as we encounter the complete, Jesus tells us that we have help. God sends the Holy Spirit to us to remind us of his words, to help us understand his words, and to bear his words. He helps us to embrace the complete, and he helps effect a marriage between the complete and the incomplete. The Spirit of God helps enfold the completeness of the relationship between the Father and the Son into the incompleteness of our own imaginations, lives, relationships, and interactions with one another. This is the peace that he gives. It is not a peace that the world gives because the world is incomplete and still emerging. The peace that God gives is complete and eternal.

The Gospel of John creates a dialogue in our imaginations between the complete and the incomplete, between the temporal and the contingent on the one hand and the eternal on the other.

When Jesus returns to the Father, their relationship becomes complete. When we open our imaginations to their relationship, their relationship is enfolded into our imaginations. When we open our relationships with one another to the relationship between the Father and the Son, their relationship unfolds in our dialogue. Our relationships, which are incomplete and still emerging, begin to unfold in the relationship between God and Christ. As our relationships unfold, they are enfolded into the mystery of their completeness. We become whole.

INSIGHT FROM MATTHEW

*The nature of this one Reality is such that it cannot be directly
and immediately apprehended except by those who have chosen to
fulfill certain conditions, making themselves loving, pure in heart,
and poor in Spirit.*

—Aldous Huxley, quoted in Joseph Jaworski, *Source*

Matthew's insights are every bit as astonishing as those of
Mark, Luke, and John. He may not have been the first to
see the strong connection between the words and actions
of Jesus and Moses, but he was the single Gospel writer who developed
those connections into a poetic whole that makes it possible for us to
know and understand their vitality. Matthew makes the interconnections
between Jesus and Moses accessible—easy to recognize. This isn't, as we
are wont to say, rocket science.

The Gospel begins with Joseph, the betrothed husband of Mary,
and this is a direct allusion to Joseph, the son of Jacob, who is the last
major figure of the book of Genesis (see Genesis 37—50). Just as Joseph
son of Jacob sets the stage for Moses, the actions of Joseph betrothed

the Sermon on the Mount, after which I will say something about the relationship between Moses's striking the rock, from which water gushes forth (Exodus 17), and the Parable of the Treasure Hidden in the Field. At their most obvious level, the realities linking the plagues with the ten miracles involve the issue of tearing down and building up—de-creation and creation. The backdrop for the ten plagues in Exodus is the creation story in Genesis 1. Like with the Genesis story, the plagues begin with water. The difference is that whereas water becomes an instrument and source of creation in Genesis 1, the water in Exodus, so to speak, bleeds, becoming an instrument of death. And the creatures that emerge from the waters in the second plague—frogs—are, from the perspective of Genesis 1, an anomaly. The creatures represented in Genesis 1 each have a clear association of place, which also provides a basis for the dietary laws in Leviticus. God creates fish for the water, birds for the air, animals and humans for the land. The creatures involved in the plagues are frogs, gnats, and flies, none of which are mentioned in Genesis 1. Instead of being the fruits of creativity, they are the cause of affliction for the Egyptians. The only creatures from the creation story that are mentioned are livestock and humans, but they are victims, not instruments, of the plague. They are all subject to boils and sores, hail, infestation by locusts, and finally, death. The creative action of the breath of God, light, and life, all of which are essential to the Genesis story, are the backdrop for their destructive opposites in Exodus. Whereas the breath of God blows over the deep, fathomless abyss in Genesis 1, the wind blows swarms of locusts which infest the land in Exodus. Whereas God says, "Let there be light," which shines as the source of creativity in Genesis, flashes of lightening accompany the hail, which hammers the Egyptians. Whereas the climax of the first day of creation involves the gift of light, the Egyptians are plagued by darkness. And whereas God creates humans in his own image—male and female—on the sixth day, the angel of death slaughters the firstborn of all Egyptians in the final plague. The crescendo of creation in Genesis 1 serves as the backdrop for the plagues, allowing us to understand that they are not only destructive, but de-creative. This establishes the context in which we can understand the nature of Pharaoh's hardness of heart: the enslavement and oppression of people is an assault not only on the people themselves, but also the benevolent forces of creation. This is the kind of circumstance that the ten miracles of Jesus are designed to address, resolve, and heal.

For us to understand the ten miracles, it is essential that we observe that the miracles are not stand-alone marvels, though they certainly contain or embody marvel. Matthew reveals meaning in the miracles poetically in his grouping them together in an order in which he alone places them, along with the words of Jesus—his teaching—that strategically accompany the miracles. Matthew's poetic insight allows us to recognize that Jesus's teaching and miracles are enfolded into one another, creating a larger interconnected whole, which is their meaning. Matthew's poetic creativity builds on the astounding insight of Mark, which Matthew both treasures on its own terms and then renders all the richer for the time and reflection that he has given to them in the composition of his Gospel.

The ten miracles (Matthew 8—9) begin with the Healing of the Leper, who would have been considered an anomaly and sent into exile for his uncleanness (see Leviticus 13—14). In his willingness to touch and to heal the leper, Jesus is healing both his affliction (the function of a plague) and the anomaly, which was the rationale for his exile. By healing the leper, Jesus restores both his health and his membership in the community. This is followed by the healing of the slave of the centurion (a Gentile Roman). This miracle is for a person the lowest of social standing who is enslaved to an enemy of Israel. And yet, in spite of his relationship to Israel, the humanity of this unnamed centurion is as admirable as the Samaritan, who is the subject of the parable in Luke's Gospel and the window in the Cathedral of Chartres. This centurion honors the personhood and dignity of a man whom he might otherwise consider as mere property, unworthy of personal consideration. Whereas we who read this story will find the healing of the slave to be the marvel, Jesus finds marvel in the attitude and actions of the centurion: he holds the best interests of both his slave and Jesus at heart. The centurion wants healing for his slave, and at the same time, he wants not to be an imposition on Jesus. The centurion also wants his request not to inconvenience Jesus. And he cares far more for the well-being of his slave than for the prestige of being seen with Jesus. This centurion wants things to go well for both Jesus and the slave in need of Jesus's healing. This is the marvel within the marvel.

Jesus then heals many others, including the mother-in-law of Peter. These first three miracles set the stage for Jesus's first teaching, which focuses on the cost of following him—a decision that requires all of the resolve that a would-be follower can muster. These words calling for total tenacity are enfolded in the miracle that follows—the calming of the storm, which embodies the adversity and difficulty that Jesus's followers face. Jesus and his disciples get into a boat for a journey across the Sea of Galilee, where they are hammered by a storm which swamps them with waves, provoking terror in the hearts of the disciples. Jesus calms the storm, chastising the disciples for their lack of faith. The Calming of the Storm allows us to experience the resolve necessitated in the follower, who is confronted by storms from without and is met by the confident power of Christ as calming presence.

Like in the Gospel of Mark, immediately following the Calming of the Storm, Jesus and his disciples proceed to the country of the Gadarenes. But in Matthew's Gospel, they are confronted not by one demoniac, but two. We will see a similar phenomenon in the ninth miracle, where Jesus heals *two* blind men, as opposed to Mark's one. What is Matthew showing us? The purging of evil and learning to see are not solely individual events. They are deeply personal, but they lead to communion. The need for exorcism may involve individuals, or it may involve relationships and communities. For us to be in communion with one another, it is essential that we allow Christ to address the evil that blinds *us*. And that is because righteousness—having a solid rock on which to stand—is not a merely private matter, though it certainly reaches to who we are and what we do when no one is looking. Righteousness includes our interaction with others, including sustained thought leading to action that is essential in securing for others their due as children of God—people of uncompromised dignity.

Matthew's miracles—including their order—take an interesting route following the exorcism of the two men possessed by demons. Whereas in Mark's Gospel, Jesus heals the paralytic immediately following his healing the leper, in Matthew's Gospel, the Healing of the Paralytic follows the Healing of the Demoniacs. We saw in Mark's Gospel that Jesus's offering the forgiveness of sins to the paralytic provoked serious objections on behalf of the scribes. We also saw how the splitting open of the roof of Jesus's house with the descent of the paralytic is connected to the splitting open of the heavens and the descent of the dove at Jesus's baptism. In Matthew, there is no splitting open of the roof. Matthew does, however, retain the centrality and importance of Jesus's authority and willingness to forgive sin (to which the scribes still object). At the same time, Matthew uncovers new insight into these miracles, which he composes for us to behold. The Healing of the Paralytic is followed by a confrontation. Jesus calls Matthew, a tax collector, and other sinners, who come to Jesus for hospitality, which Jesus offers them. This outrages the Pharisees, prompting Jesus to respond that it is those who are sick who are in need of a physician. This is followed by an encounter between Jesus and the disciples of John the Baptist, who want to know why Jesus enjoys feasting instead of fasting. Jesus responds with an analogy from the wedding: the guests do not fast as long as the bridegroom is present. He adds that no one sews an un-shrunk patch on an old garment (this will cause a tear) and no one pours new wine into old, brittle wineskins (this will cause them to tear and burst). Matthew is showing us that the miracles that Jesus is enacting are causing old, brittle wineskins to tear and burst. The realities that are unfolding in his interaction with others are so vital and astonishing that they are for wineskins that are receptive because they are supple.

This insight uncovers new meaning in the story of the Healing of the Woman with the Hemorrhage. When we looked at this story in Mark's Gospel, we saw how Mark recognized the apocalyptic quality of this story: just as the heavens split open when Jesus is baptized, and just as the followers of Jesus split open the roof of Jesus's house, so does Jesus's encounter with the woman split open the story of the Healing of Jairus's Daughter. As in Mark, the story of the woman with the hemorrhage is contained within the story of the healing of a twelve year old girl; but in Matthew's Gospel, there are one or two differences. First, the man who approaches Jesus to request healing for his daughter is not a ruler of the *synagogue*, but merely "a ruler," who kneels before Jesus. This raises a question in our imaginations. Instead of being associated with Israel, is this ruler associated with Gentiles (like the centurion)? The second thing that we notice by way of comparison is that the age of the ruler's daughter is not mentioned (in Mark's Gospel, she is twelve years old). Matthew's story seems to suggest a diminishing connection with Israel in the synagogue. Why is this so? Matthew's insight is that the healing of the woman with the hemorrhage is the new wine that is poured into the place in need of healing—the household of the ruler that is receptive and hospitable—like a wineskin that is supple, ready to receive new wine without rupturing or bursting. The marvel of new wine is the wonder of forgiveness leading to communion, and it is offered freely to the open and receptive. The new wine of forgiveness is what leads to justice and righteousness in the community. This is the reality that merits insight and conversation: the final two miracles are first the healing of *two* blind men, and then the healing of the man who is mute. Why are there two blind men in Matthew as opposed to one in Mark? They are connected to the two demoniacs that Jesus exorcises. The ability to see, which leads to insight, is deeply personal, but not individualistic. The end of learning to see is communion. This is the matter that merits conversation and dialogue, and this is why the healing of the mute follows and accompanies the healing of the blind. They go hand-in-hand.

This kind of insight also makes possible our recognizing the interconnections between the ten miracles in Matthew and the ten plagues in the Exodus. The hard, brittle wineskins in Matthew are connected to the hardness of heart in Pharaoh. Objections to forgiveness, to enfolding tax collectors and sinners into the communion of the people of God, reflect Pharaoh's harsh treatment of the Hebrew slaves. This kind of harshness is akin to the de-creation of the world. The willful affliction of slaves leads to the affliction of plagues. The power that Jesus embodies meets the marvel of the supple wineskins that are the lives of the leper, the centurion, the paralytic, the woman with the hemorrhage, tax collectors, and other sinners. The power that Jesus embodies prepares a people receptive and hospitable. In a word, the power that Jesus embodies prepares hearts at peace in people who are spiritually impoverished.

Matthew begins serious preparations for our ability to recognize this reality in the Sermon on the Mount (Matthew 5—7). The Sermon begins with a most curious beatitude, "Blessed are the poor of spirit; theirs is the kingdom of heaven." This single sentence is marvel: it calls into our imaginations a gap between poverty of spirit on the one hand and inheritance of the kingdom of heaven—the whole world of God's sovereignty—on the other. We don't tend to think of the spiritually impoverished as heirs of the kingdom of heaven; we tend to think of those who are spiritually rich. Examples might include Mother Teresa, Billy Graham, Martin Luther King Jr., Pope John Paul II, John Wesley, and Nelson Mandela. These are people who have embodied readily recognizable goodness and self-evident communion with God and with people. On the other hand, the suggestion that people who are spiritually impoverished inherit the kingdom of heaven is at the very least cause for curiosity: how is this so? How is it that people who clearly lack spiritual substance inherit the kingdom of heaven? What is it that fills the undeniable gap between our spiritual poverty and the kingdom of heaven?

The Gospel of Matthew doesn't rely on propositions: he doesn't *tell* us the answer. Matthew shows us. Learning to see precedes learning to speak; the healing of the blind precedes the healing of the mute. I think that the reason for this is that when we *learn* to see, the ability to see is our own: it becomes second nature. I also think that learning to recognize sources of spiritual riches makes it possible for us to return to those riches when we find ourselves in times and places of spiritual dryness, which are part and parcel of our humanity, which is incomplete and always unfolding. To put this another way, learning to see makes it possible for us to take responsibility for enfolding the insights that Matthew shows us into our own sovereign imaginations for our own embodiment and living.

What Matthew shows us is nothing short of a marvel, and one of Matthew's unique marvels is nothing if not short. The thirteenth chapter of the Gospel is a composition of parables, which begins to come to conclusion with the Parable of the Treasure Hidden in the Field. Jesus likens the kingdom of heaven to a treasure, which is hidden in a field, which a man, having found, covers up, departs, sells all of his possessions, returns, and purchases the entire field. This parable provides an observational feast that is inversely proportional to the length of the parable, which is a mere two sentences; and what we can observe leads not so much to direct answers as to more questions. It's as though the effect of the design of the parable is to send us on a kind of scavenger hunt. We know that a man finds a treasure. We don't know who he is, nor do we know the identity of the owner of the field. We don't know if the man was trespassing, and we don't know what he actually did to the field. Did the man in search of treasure know where the treasure was buried? Did X mark the spot? If not, did he have to dig several holes to find the treasure? And if so, did he leave the field looking as though it were infested by moles? And what about the owner of the field: did he know about the treasure? I presume that he did not because he willingly sold the field. This raises the question of moral obligation on the part of the buyer: was he under obligation to tell the owner about the treasure? And speaking of the treasure, what was it? How much was it worth? And how much was the man who purchased the field worth? What was the value of his liquid net assets?

Jesus's parable provokes these questions in our imaginations, and it does so without providing the answers at this point, halfway through the Gospel. Still, Matthew shows us that there is much to see, especially if we are willing to scan the horizon of the Gospel in both directions. When we place the Parable of the Treasure Hidden in the Field alongside the first beatitude, what do we notice? How are they connected? Both portray a gap. The gap in the beatitude involves acres of distance between spiritual poverty and the kingdom of heaven. When we read this beatitude, we become aware of our own spiritual poverty and wonder how the gap is bridged or filled: how is it that we, who know ourselves to be spiritually impoverished, find the wherewithal to inherit the world of God's sovereign love and righteousness? How is it that our spiritual poverty enjoys a connection with the kingdom of heaven?

The answer begins to emerge in the parable, where Jesus shows us another gap. This gap is a hole in the earth, which contains the treasure. We don't yet know what the treasure is, but the parable cultivates the kind of curiosity that activates our imaginations and causes us to ponder the connections between the parable and the beatitude. It suggests that the connection between an awareness of our spiritual poverty and the kingdom of heaven is a treasure of invaluable import that merits every ounce of insight of which our imaginations are capable.

What might the treasure be? Again, Matthew doesn't tell us; he shows us. When we arrive at the twenty-seventh chapter, where Matthew makes us witnesses of the crucifixion of Jesus, he shows us matters that are unique to Matthew's poetic composition. Matthew, and Matthew alone, features earth and rock. As he brings us to the climax and conclusion of his Gospel, Matthew has been using the substance of rock and earth as expressions of the solidity of justice and righteousness—finding solid ground on which to stand. When Jesus is crucified in the Gospel of Matthew, the earth quakes, rocks split, tombs open up, and saints who have died rise from the dead and appear in the holy city. When Jesus is then buried, Matthew emphasizes his being buried in a new tomb that is cut in rock, with a great stone rolled to seal the entrance. And when, on the first day of the week, Jesus rises from the dead, there is a great earthquake, caused by the descent from heaven of the angel of the Lord, who rolled back the stone from the tomb. These details are all that we need to see—to recognize that the treasure hidden in the field that fills the gap of our spiritual poverty and fits us for the kingdom of heaven is the power by which God raised Christ from the dead. The power by which God raised Christ is the treasure hidden in the field. This is the power that takes those of us who know ourselves to be spiritually impoverished and makes us spiritually rich. This is the power that transforms us into the fullness of human dignity. The power by which God raised Christ from the dead is the same power that transforms the gall of transgression into the wine of forgiveness leading to communion in justice and love.

When Moses, following the directions of God, brought the Hebrew people out of slavery and oppression in Egypt, he took them across the dry riverbed of the Red Sea into the Wilderness. It was not easy going, and the people were not always grateful for their deliverance. As humans are wont to do, the people of Israel grumbled, moaned, and flat-out complained. By the time they set up camp at Rephidim, there was no water. The people were understandably thirsty, and they let Moses know, in no terms uncertain, that they were anything but happy campers. Moses took the people's complaint to God, and God responded by telling Moses he would stand before Moses on the rock of Horeb. Moses was to take the staff with which he struck the Nile and strike the rock, from which water would gush forth. Moses did so in the sight of the elders of Israel, and the people recognized the presence of God. The water that flowed wasn't the bleeding, poisonous water of the first plague; it was fresh, living water to quench the parched throats of a thirsty people.

Matthew has composed a Gospel which makes it possible for us to see the connection between the water that flowed from the rock and the treasure hidden in the field. In Christ, the water that flows from the rock is the power by which God raised Christ from the dead. This is the power that fills the gaps of spiritual poverty in our lives. This is how we come to communion in love, which makes us whole, new, and just. This is how we are fit for the kingdom of heaven.

THE ORIGIN OF
MY BIRTHPLACE

We are such stuff
As dreams are made on, and our little life
Is rounded with a sleep.
      —William Shakespeare, *The Tempest*

All is like an ocean, all is flowing and blending; a touch in one
place sets up movement at the other end of the earth.
      —Father Zossima, in Fyodor Dostoevsky,
                  The Brothers Karamazov

I n Dante's Divine Comedy, Dante the pilgrim works his way up
Mount Purgatory, during which he is cleansed (purged) of the
Seven Deadly Sins—Pride, Envy, Wrath, Sloth, Avarice, Gluttony,
and Lust. Purged of these sins, he enters earthly Paradise, the Garden
of Eden. There, he encounters a pageant of learning and meets Beatrice.
She is the one who cared enough about Dante and his being lost, midway

through his life, in a dark wood. Beatrice is the one who dispatched Virgil to guide Dante through Hell and Purgatory, where he would learn about his own sin and shortcomings and be made fit to explore Paradise, where Beatrice will be Dante's guide. Before Dante makes the journey through the heavens, he is made witness to the pageant of learning. A Griffin enters earthly Paradise, drawing a car on which sits seven women who embody the seven virtues—faith, hope, love, temperance, prudence, courage, and justice.

There are many things about Dante's insight that are rich beyond measure. Two are particularly important for our explorations into the world of primary knowing. I will begin with Beatrice's observations of the Griffin, which is a cross between a lion and an eagle. The Griffin is a metaphor for the incarnation—Christ, who is both fully human and fully divine. Dante's *Divine Comedy* is about learning to see. Dante the poet shows us Beatrice as she observes the Griffin. As she does so, Dante the pilgrim looks into her eyes. What he sees astonishes him. In one of her eyes, Dante sees reflected a fully formed lion. In the other, he sees reflected a fully formed eagle. Dante comes to a primary knowing: he comes to understand that when Beatrice observes the Griffin, she sees both a lion in its completeness and an eagle in its completeness. The paradox is that she sees them as one. In Beatrice, as in Christ, the interconnections are complete.

The second matter for Dante's experience is equally important and bears insight that is connected to the windows in the Cathedral of Chartres. Two of the windows portray the crucifixion of Christ. One is a lancet window on the West Wall; the other is the Redemption Window. In both, the cross on which Christ is crucified is green. It is green because of a legend that was at large in the Middle Ages: the wood from the cross on which Christ was crucified came from the Tree of the Knowledge of Good and Evil from the Garden of Eden. In Dante's earthly Paradise, on the car drawn by the Griffin is the pole on which Christ was crucified. Dante makes us witnesses as the pole is rejoined to the Tree of Knowledge. As the two are connected, the pole of crucifixion bursts into full flower.

Dante the poet draws us into communion with his own primary knowing. In the presence of the Griffin, the eyes of Beatrice, and the green pole joined to the Tree of Knowledge, we observe the wholeness of primary knowing. Connections are everything. It is in the connections between disparate parts that meaning comes to flourish. Seeing connections and making connections, we enter into the heart of generativity and life itself. Meaning and communion are found in the wonder and marvel of interconnected wholes. They are ever present for us to see; they are ever present for us to make.

The two dreams that were a gift to me showed me that this is a reality that is part and parcel to my soul. When I saw the image of the sky-blue ocean which was being ever penetrated by the pure-white breath of God, I was given the gift of seeing that within all of us is embedded the Source of Life—the expanse of generativity in which and from which God ever breathes life. My second, complementary dream was pure voice: *I keep taking something fresh to the origin of my birthplace.* Both dreams were so clear that I could immediately, upon emerging from sleep, write them in my journal. I was then captivated by a knowing: it is my responsibility to take the pieces and material of my own experience and circumstances to the origin of my birthplace, which is embodied in the dream of the sky-blue deep, over which the breath of God blows and penetrates my being. Deep calls unto deep; and I am responsible for taking the stuff of life to the origin.

I found it important to observe that the wisdom of the dream told me actually *to take* the material, events, and circumstances of life to the origin of my birthplace. I also found it essential to observe that the dream wasn't calling me to take the stuff of life to my birthplace. The foundational insight was that my birthplace has a Source—an Origin. The paradox is that the origin is both within and without—it is located both in the inside and in the expanse of the heavens. It is ever present for communion; it is ever open to receiving the material and fruit of my imagination, will, and action. I am responsible for recognizing, forging, and remembering the vital connections between the circumstances of life, my imagination, my will, and the origin of my birthplace. It is in those connections, for which I am responsible, that life unfolds and possibilities and opportunities come to flourish.

In order to be mindful of, create, and maintain a world of interconnected wholes, I came to a series of complementary insights that it is my joy to share. For me, these insights are essential. That said, each person is responsible for developing his or her own insights.

It is essential that I see people as people. When I look at a human being, I cannot afford to see the person as an object. When I do so, I not only de-humanize the person, but I also de-humanize myself. I have to be vigilant in my willingness to see people as people and to respond to people as people. Only then can I connect with people as they are—as fully human. I also find it essential that I look for the best in people, observe the best in people, and respond to what is best. There are plenty of others who will take care of responding to what is worst in others, and I am happy to leave that to them. In my experience, people can be their best if I will work at seeing what is best in them. I am fully aware that there are occasions when I must be "wise as serpents." In giving the gift of seeing others at their best, I can help create a climate in which communion unfolds.

Becoming comfortable with silence has been critical to my own journey. I have to work at de-cluttering my mind. I do so through meditation. I try to take myself to the place within where there is little, if any, thought. I recently had the opportunity to enter a sensory deprivation tank, where I would float in complete darkness and silence for over an hour. This helped me to clear my mind and to enjoy absolute silence. Because I wore ear plugs, the only sound I could hear while floating in darkness was the sound of my breathing, which sounds very much like the waves of the ocean washing up on the shore.

I find meditation to be a treasure, just as I find prayer to be a treasure. Interacting with God in silence helps me to be mindful of God when I am interacting with people.

Curiosity is an essential path to primary knowing and communion. Curiosity is also an invaluable asset of the human spirit. This does not mean that I should follow my curiosity everywhere it takes me. A wise measure of prudence is essential. There is such a thing as indulging curiosity in ways that can be counter-productive or even destructive. I have found it helpful to cultivate curiosity by directing it towards creativity, generativity, life, art, literature, music, communion, love, peace, joy, justice, and righteousness. I have also found it helpful to think of love, peace, and joy as metaphysical substance. This kind of imagination leads to all kinds of openings.

We are all responsible for committing to truth. When we commit to truth, it opens a dialogue within the human heart, and when groups commit to truth, it opens a dialogue among us where truth emerges and unfolds. I have found that no single person has a corner on truth or knows the truth in any exhaustive fashion. I have found that when we are committed to and open to truth, we can listen to one another as fellow humans and that new meaning and truth unfold in our midst.

In this same vein, we are all responsible for recognizing connections and learning to see the larger interconnected whole. We all bear the capacity to see whole processes from germination to metabolism to emerging to unfolding to developing to growth to fruition and to death, which provides seeds for the germination of new life. It is important to be mindful, as much as we are able, of whole processes.

Humility is an essential for our capacity to understand truth and to see interconnected wholes. Things go best when I am willing to set aside my assumptions, presumptions, and compulsion to be seen as right. My belief that I have to look good and to be seen as omni-competent can be the very blinder to recognizing truth and seeing connections. There are times when the knowledge we cling to becomes the roadblock to primary knowing. It is good to learn to lay aside assumptions as a matter of habit.

The Hebrews are important for many reasons, not the least of which is that they sought to know God directly in the concrete circumstances of their life together. The Hebrews recognized that communion with God and one another is everything—the very reason for life itself. Abraham was the first to understand this fully. In him, we are witnesses as a human life comes into the competence of full awareness of the presence of God, including ways in which God is present. Abraham's imagination comes to a more or less complete awareness of the presence of the power of God in deliverance. The descendants of Abraham continued to be aware of this presence and to wrestle with this to the benefit of the entire world. It is self-evident that communion is the end of life, the reason for our existence. We are, first and last, an interconnected whole. The Hebrews also understood that mystery is ever-present in the concrete circumstances of life, and the exploration of mystery is a supremely worthy undertaking. Mystery is not only ever-present, but it is also its own reward; it renders life rich in meaning and authenticity.

In engaging God, the Hebrews didn't so much spend time explaining God or theorizing about God, but knowing God in the hard, concrete circumstances of their lives. Explanations *about* God were not nearly as important as *knowing* God. It is self-evident that this is also true for human relationships. It is better to know people and to interact with people than it is to analyze and to explain people. It is self-evident that communion is its own reward.

We easily forget—at least, I do. Remembrance is critical. It was for Abraham; it was for Jesus: "Do this in remembrance of me." Abraham built an altar because he recognized not only that he needed to remember God and his experience with God, but his acts of remembering provided the means for the metaphysical formatting of his life. This is why he built altars. Jesus provided for the metaphysical formatting of life in The Lord's Supper and The Lord's Prayer. Remembering matters of the greatest import can be difficult. Occasions for remembering and means of remembrance help re-enkindle the flame of primary knowing, creativity, and communion.

These kinds of movements of spirit open us up to the insight of primary knowing. I have found that this clears the underbrush that lays bare the fertile soil in which the four Gospels cultivated their insight. I have also found that the insights of Matthew, Mark, Luke, and John, who are perched on the shoulders of prophets in the South Window, make it possible for us to see farther as well.

From Mark and Melchizedek, we see the connections between bread and wine and deliverance. Mark shows us that Jesus took the astonishing step of enfolding insight into deliverance into the bread with the words, *take, this is my body, given for you.* This opens our eyes to possible ways that we can split open and transfigure our own circumstances by identifying possibilities in which we might transform our own being taken into a gracious gift. In small ways, we can begin to embody what Christ embodied in the great transformation of the Lord's Supper. When we embody the actions of Christ, this is a kind of primary knowing. We begin to learn how to sense, internalize, and act on the presence of tenderness even amidst harshness and cruelty.

From Luke, we can begin to recognize that Christ actually joins us in our captivity. When we are held hostage to circumstances or disposition to sin or to hostilities, Christ is present and willing to take us to that place of inner knowing, the source of life, the origin of our birthplace. Luke also understands the importance of remembrance. Luke understands that we can have difficulty remembering and that we need to build occasions and opportunities for remembrance so that we can persevere in communion with one another and the source of life.

John understood, perhaps better than anyone, that the Father and the Son form the primary relationship in which we ourselves can participate. It is one of the great metaphysical mysteries. The Father enfolds the Son into himself. The Father and the Son pour forth their communion into our lives, and this enfolds us into their eternal communion. This communion constitutes the origin of our birthplace, the source of life. This is the place where we go in the landscape and topography of our imaginations. This is also the place to which we take people through the action of prayer.

Matthew shows us the paradox of our own internal suppleness with the hunger and thirst for justice and righteousness. The paradox begins with the recognition that righteousness involves finding a solid place on which to stand. At the same time, the key to receptivity isn't to be hard on the inside, but to host a certain agility and nimbleness of imagination. That's where God can pour in the new wine that transforms that need for justice into the marvel of togetherness. The new wine of justice is the marvel of forgiveness. This is the cask from which we drink in heady new opportunities and possibilities for togetherness, wholeness, and communion.

Matthew, Mark, Luke, and John each portray insight into the meaning of the life, death, and resurrection of Christ. Their insights provide openings—portholes to the oceans of primary knowing. They help us to recognize that entering into communion with God and with the unfolding order of the world is a matter of imagination and human willingness. With Abraham, the four Gospel writers recognized that faith includes measures of trust and obedience, but is not blind. Faith is a matter of such comprehensive breadth that it contains whole worlds of contents. For Abraham, this includes the power by which God delivers people from intolerable circumstances into opportunities for creativity and wholeness. For the four evangelists, this includes the ways in which the power by which God raised Christ from the dead unfolds in the circumstances of our lives, bringing us into opportunities for new creativity and communion.

All of this is built on the metaphysical premise that the world is permeated with a Source of life—the origin of our birthplace, which is enfolded into every part, every fragment of the world, binding the

THE LABYRINTH

This is as strange a maze as e'er men trod
And there is in this business more than nature
Was ever conduct of: some oracle
Must rectify our knowledge.
    —William Shakespeare, *The Tempest*

And again this was not utterly strange, but like the resumption
of something once cherished, and lost for a time.
    —Robertson Davies, *A Mixture of Frailties*

Because it was a Friday, the chairs in the Cathedral of Chartres had been drawn back and were neatly placed in rows around the Labyrinth. On Fridays, pilgrims walk.

On this particular Friday, as I approach the Labyrinth, I observe a woman standing in the center. She faces the West Wall with its Rose Window and its three lancets in a gesture hieratic. Other pilgrims walk the Labyrinth. A couple stands at the edge of the center with their arms around each other. The woman whom I first noticed in the center begins her return walk. She does so with complete deliberation and balance, placing one foot in front of the other with her arms carefully at the side. She raises one foot slowly off the path with her toe pointed downward, extends the foot forward, and places her foot gently and firmly on the path. She then raises the other knee, drawing her other foot up. As her foot is held above the path, she pauses with her toe pointed downward. She shifts the foot forward and continues her walk.

The Labyrinth has many turns. At each, the woman pauses and makes the turn with care. From time to time, the woman again pauses in a gesture hieratic. She possesses a knowing, and the knowing is enfolded into her. Again, with forethought, the woman continues her journey.

A man is making his walk with care. His gestures are his own. He has folded his hands in front of himself, and he places one foot slowly in front of the other, with the heal of the foot in front touching the toe of the other. When he comes to a turn in the Labyrinth, he places his feet, heal to toe, at right angles.

Another woman takes longer steps, but she takes hers in pairs, pausing between each for reflection and contemplation. When she approaches the center, she gains a bit of momentum, as if arriving at her destination, the center, has understandably overcome her with joy.

As my attention returns to the first woman, who walks with self-possession and the grace of a dancer, I consider photographing her. The Cathedral is a public place. But a second thought visits the sovereignty of my imagination: this woman is on a journey in this moment in this place here and now. This is not something in which I care to intrude. My opportunity and my choice are to watch and to honor this deeply personal journey. For what I see—what I witness—reminds me of deep calling unto deep. As the woman comes to a turn in the Labyrinth, she momentarily breaks with her dance. A man approaches her. She makes room for him to pass as he moves in the opposite direction towards the center.

I am sitting on the perimeter of the Labyrinth. She is now approaching the place where I am sitting, and I will watch as she passes by. The woman's face conveys a focused, un-tense, satisfying joy. When another pilgrim approaches, the woman respectfully stands to the side of the narrow path, acknowledging the presence of a fellow traveler. The other pilgrim passes by.

There are at this moment four pilgrims in the Labyrinth. Each walks with his or her own characteristic consideration. When a pilgrim passes the man who walks heal to toe, he moves his hands up to his chest palm to palm and honors the passing pilgrim. His honor embodies the recognition that the fellow traveler, who moves at a different pace, is equally precious.

Others now enter the Labyrinth. Their own walks are rapid, informal, and comparatively clumsy, conveying the impression of tourists whose visit to the Cathedral is like visiting a theme park. They walk the Labyrinth rapidly, sloppily, and without any evidence of mindfulness. In other words, they do not measure their steps. It appears that their goal is less to savor the moment and more to get it over with. They will be able to tell others, "I toured the Cathedral, and I walked the Labyrinth" and check it off their list. For them it was more of a sprint than a journey of reflection and contemplation. They got it over and done with as fast as possible and were out of there: *Zoom, zoom, zoom! I came, I walked, and I went to the gift shop!*

This is not the case with the woman who dances. For her, the Labyrinth is a treasure. In the slowness of her walk, she recovers something once cherished. It is clear that she actively cherishes every measured movement and every measured step, all of which she connects in her imagination.

As the woman approaches the last leg of her journey, the man who walks with his own deliberation passes her in the opposite direction. He stops, raises his hands to the level of his heart, palms pressed together, and honors the woman. She also stops and does likewise. After he passes, the woman pauses facing the West Rose Window in a final hieratic gesture. Her meditation takes her to the lancet windows—The Jesse Window, The Incarnation Window, and the Passion and Resurrection. The woman welcomes these works into the awareness of her imagination. As she reaches the entrance to the Labyrinth, which is now her point of departure, she recapitulates the entire experience. She returns to a chair, prays, puts on her shoes, writes in her journal, sits, and reflects. The woman is taking all of it in. She is receiving the experience in the sovereignty of her imagination. She appears satisfied. In some visible sense, her wholeness is intact.

I have witnessed a knowing which is primary. I have observed deep calling unto deep. We are all at the origin of our birthplace. That I have observed. This I know.

APPENDIX

OBSTACLES TO PRIMARY KNOWING

B ecause I believe in the importance of primary knowing, I think it important to address the challenge of obstacles. I don't believe that primary knowing is a matter of technique or mechanics. There is no surefire, foolproof recipe to primary knowing. Primary knowing is not something that we "figure out" or conquer once and for all. It isn't a theory or formula. Primary knowing isn't a matter of mechanics or technique. But I do think that there are obstacles to primary knowing. I think we can recognize these obstacles both from personal experience and from great literature and art. I also think that we are wise to be mindful of the ways we are actually approaching life. Learning something about the obstacles to primary knowing is not complicated. Obstacles are fairly easy to identify because they are fairly obvious. I do not intend the list that follows to be exhaustive. I do hope that it will open awareness into the obstacles that we tend to nurture or hang on to. What follows is a brief description of obstacles to primary knowing that are common. In the following essay, we will look at pathways to primary knowing.

A key obstacle to primary knowing involves our willingness to break the bonds of human trust, tenderness, and communion. People are treasures. The world of connections is a treasure. God is a treasure. Conflict is all but inevitable. Because of this, we are wise to anticipate conflict with others. We cannot, however, afford to allow our human conflicts to undermine or break our human bonds. We live in a world that is interconnected, and the bonds of tenderness and communion are essential. These bonds lie of the intersections of primary knowing.

The breaking of human bonds leads to exploitation, factionalism, isolation, and despair. Any of these can become a black hole that consumes and drains our energy, including our desire for knowing that is primary. When we break human bonds, we are in danger of betraying those who trust us. Exploiting others becomes more likely. We can become willing to punish others for sins for which we ourselves are guilty. Isolation is so painful that we all too often react by defending isolation through rationalization. Legitimating and defending isolation lead to factionalism which causes even more hardening. Hard boundaries lead to hard hearts. We not only react with defensiveness, but we also run the risk of becoming sullen, angry, and lost in despair. We become more vulnerable to going after each other, attacking each other with recriminations, and being unwilling to see our own role in causing isolation, anger, and despair. Unwilling to suffer hurt and pain, we become all too willing to cause pain in others.

A second serious obstacle to primary knowing is obsessive self-indulgence. When indulging ourselves becomes our single focus or reason for living, the satisfaction of our desires becomes its own drug. We refuse to embrace reasonable limits and mutually beneficial boundaries. We become unreasonable, and we rationalize and defend our hunger for the satisfaction of desire. We begin to imagine that we need to experience everything, without regard for consequences to self and others. We then become willing to impose on others responsibilities that are properly ours. We become unwilling to do the heavy lifting that is our own responsibility. We blame others for not accepting responsibilities. The byproduct for militant self-indulgence is that we weaken and finally refuse to discern between knowledge that is worth pursuing and knowledge that destroys self, others, and the bonds of human tenderness and communion. This leads us to squander our time and energy with finger pointing, blame, and recrimination.

Our willingness to break the bonds of human communion and to persist in chronic self-indulgence creates conditions in which we easily disregard wisdom. Wisdom is intimately connected to primary knowing. It is accumulated over years of experience, thoughtful reflection, and testing. Wisdom is tried and true. It merits attention and thoughtfulness that are of a high order. It is very difficult to know and understand wisdom in pieces and fragments. Wisdom is always applied in the concrete circumstances of the here and now, but at the same time, wisdom involves the long view of the world. Becoming wise requires a fair measure of concentration, mindfulness, and perseverance. It includes the recognition that there is an accumulated knowledge for which others have paid dearly that is a treasure.

Another obstacle to primary knowing involves our attempts to use magic and to change or to manipulate the orders of nature. The processes of nature are an entire library of wisdom and knowledge. If our ways of dealing with the processes of nature are manipulative and exploitive, we run the risk of thinking ourselves entitled to determine what the processes of nature should be instead of respecting and learning from them. This is the very issue with which the Devil confronted Jesus when he said, "Turn these stones into bread." Stones and bread are of different, but complementary orders.

Believing that we have the right to manipulate and exploit the natural processes of nature leads to the belief that I have the right to manipulate and to dominate others. When I believe that I am number one, or have the right to be number one, I then believe that I am entitled to dominate and run roughshod over others. A corollary to manipulating others involves having always to do things my way, including requiring others to do things my way as well. And if people refuse to play by my rules, I then refuse to play with them. I may also refuse to recognize the existence or legitimacy of others, treating them as inferior in ways that I alone define. This attitude leads to the destruction of the bonds of human tenderness that lie at the heart of primary knowing.

A corollary to manipulating others is trying to impress others, to get others to think highly of me, or to get others to think that I am superior to them. I may do this with flattery, boasting, sensationalism, exaggeration, talking about myself in ways that are self-promoting or self-aggrandizing, or creating pseudo-events in which I portray myself as savior to a situation, if not the world. I also portray myself as superior to others when I am a gossip, especially when I create the illusion that I am an inside source while making others look bad. When I make it my practice to confess the sins and shortcomings of others, I am exalting myself while trashing their reputations. At best, trying to impress people twists the bonds of human respectfulness. Worse is when my efforts to impress others actually destroy those bonds.

There are other significant roadblocks to primary knowing. One involves refusing to live in the present. There are people of incalculable importance who have known both God and the mystery of the orders of creation in the past. Abraham is an obvious example. It is also true that our coming to understand Abraham and his story can lead to communion with God. But our own communion with God is always located right smack dab in the present. Our knowing God involves the here and now, not the there and then. There is nothing wrong with being mindful of the past, nor is there anything wrong with joining minds and hearts for the creation of a bright new future. But we are only mindful of the past and future in the present. Refusing to live in the present moment is an obstacle to active mindful primary knowing.

A corollary to refusing to live in the present involves treating parts as wholes and partial truths as the whole truth. When I treat partial truths as the whole truth, I not only misrepresent the whole, but I also break the bonds of wholeness. I may actually decompose wholeness into pieces that become mere fragments—isolated and unrelated. The history of primary knowing involves times of ecstasy and rapture that are both mysterious and wonderful. These delightful moments, however, are not the whole picture. They are of course to be remembered and even sought in prayerfulness and meditation. Times of ecstasy and rapture are to be remembered, treasured, and integrated into human thoughtfulness, understanding, will, and planning, all of which are mindful of a world of interconnected wholeness.

Paths to
Primary Knowing

I am using the phrase primary *knowing* instead of primary *knowledge*, the participle instead of the noun. I am doing so because primary *knowing* is a verb, not a noun. This means that it is completely active and engaged, not a static, finished product. This is not a difficult concept. My wife Nancy and I have been married for forty years. There is a certain amount of knowledge that I have about her, but our relationship is far better when I actively seek—on an ongoing basis—to know her as she wants to be known. A person who has never met Nancy may hear me talk about her. They may even develop some knowledge about Nancy. But knowing *about* her is different from meeting her and knowing her as she wants to be known. And the truth is, when Nancy meets people who are warm, hospitable, and respectful, she begins to open up, and they have the opportunity to know her directly.

The same is true for God. Knowing *about* God is different from knowing God as God wants to be known. Primary knowing involves the active, ongoing engagement and dialogue with God on God's terms, as God wants to be known. Primary knowing also involves active, ongoing engagement and dialogue with the world that God has created. Finally, primary knowing involves the engagement of imagination and all of our creative powers, both in dialogue with God and in dialogue with one another. Primary knowing is not private and exclusive; it is complete involvement in the deepest and most hospitable of communion.

There are pathways to primary knowing. Like with the previous essay on obstacles, I do not intend this to be an exhaustive list. I will be thrilled if you were to engage God and the orders of life God has created on your own in communion with others. Here are some pathways that I find to be important.

First, it is important to begin right where we are. Primary knowing is active and engaged, and it unfolds right where we are in the present moment. Primary knowing looks to both the past and the future, especially when it comes to creating a world that is whole and new, but it is completely centered and rooted in the here and now. Primary knowing depends on our being both centered and open. Openness is a matter of conscious choice. To state this matter another way, primary knowing begins and ends in hospitality—for God, for others, and for the orders of life. We begin by offering to God and to others the most gracious sustained welcome we can muster. Genesis 18 is helpful here: Abraham offered the most exquisite of hospitality to three strangers who, as Abraham eventually discovered, were God. Because of this hospitality, Abraham *entertained angels unaware.* Hospitality for God, for people, and for the world are essentials for active primary knowing.

What does it mean to practice hospitality for the world? This involves our respectfully recognizing that there are realities in the world— both seen and unseen—which are emerging and unfolding. They are emerging and unfolding on their own terms. They are unfolding as parts of the whole of God's artistry and design. I can know these realities through openness, humility, and respect. Knowing reality begins in kind, respectful observation, listening, and intuition.

Many of us (myself included!) are wont to meddle—to influence what is unfolding, to alter things, fix things, make adjustments, and if we are really bold, to call the shots. There are times for meddling. There are times for imagination and creativity. I don't for a minute think that God is interested in our ultimately becoming passive robots. If I believed this, I would not be in the business of education. We educate students so that they can develop their own imaginations and exercise their own creativity. That being said, there is also an aspect of primary knowing in which we are actively still, seeking to become works of art in the hands of God. Dante recognized this in his *Divine Comedy*. The penitents are purged from sin as they observe the greatest of art. So doing, they eventually become works of art, with God as the artist. In the same spirit, there are times that merit stillness, humility, and mindfulness. And lest we think we are doing nothing that matters, many a wise person has observed that our active stillness, humility, openness—our actively placing ourselves in the hands of God—reverberates throughout the world, contributing creative energy for which we are in part responsible. My own still, sustained mindfulness is of benefit to everyone.

I would like to add this about the kind of openness that is a pathway to primary knowing. We will need to be somewhat wary of theories and formulae. In my earlier years, I was not only smitten by theories and formulae, but I was adept at inflicting theories on others—especially the theories I had created. At best, I was arrogant. Worse (if we can imagine something worse than arrogance), I used my theories and formulae to define God, people, togetherness, and anything else that I regarded as targets for my theories. I measured everything and everyone with *my* theories, and I alone decided who and what were worthy, and who and what were wanting. My theories about the world defined both legitimacy and shortcomings.

There were lots of problems with this. First, God is not a theory, people are not theories, religion is not a theory, communities are not a theory, and communion is not a theory. God is mystery; people are mystery; and so are love and communion. Thankfully, I was rescued (and I hope delivered) by some important writers, including but not limited to Flannery O'Connor, Fyodor Dostoevsky, Dante, and Homer. They opened my eyes to a lot of things, including the reality that my own theories about life are not reality, and the only pathway to complete reality is complete willingness to know God, people, and the world as they actually are, not as I presume them to be.

This means that listening and observing are critical. The more we close our mouths and open our eyes and ears, the more we will step firmly onto the pathways of primary knowing. The more adept we become at knowing what we do not know and actively learning from others, the more we will enter the wonders and mysteries of primary knowing.

Primary knowing involves active openness to mystery. This does not mean that we park our brains or volunteer for lobotomies. Primary knowing is neither unreasonable nor irrational. Instead, primary knowing embraces both reason and mystery. Neither gets short-changed; both are essential. Primary knowing embraces reason and mystery as complementary. It accepts and grows comfortable with the truth that there are things that can be known by one or the other as friends. Some matters are better known by reason; others are better known as mystery. When it comes to primary knowing, it is important that we understand that primary knowing is not so much a problem or puzzle to be solved, but a mystery to be explored, experienced, lived, and treasured without hoarding and without excluding other people from our communion with mystery. Primary knowing involves actively seeking to know God as God wants to be known and actively seeking to know people and the world as they are willing to open up and disclose themselves.

At the heart of primary knowing is the world of interconnected wholes. This involves our actively recognizing that everything is connected. Every part is part of an interconnected whole, and the interconnected whole is what gives meaning to parts. We can expect interconnected wholes to be intellectually and spiritually challenging. There are interconnected wholes that are complex. This does not, however, mean that interconnected wholes are necessarily complicated. There is a difference between complexity and complication. The former embodies beauty, truth, and mystery. The latter, complication, is fraught with conflict and confusion. Mystery is to be explored in all of its inexhaustible beauty and wonder. Because mystery is infinite in its delectation, it is something that we never come to the end of.

Because primary knowing and mystery involve interconnected wholes, the bonds of human community are everything. Our connectedness as humans embodies primary knowing. Our openness to one another embodies primary knowing, and when we are actively aware of this, our capacity for primary knowing deepens.

The relationship between parts and wholes is critical. Primary knowing involves the recognition that the whole is enfolded in each of the parts. This means that our involvement with the part can also include mindfulness of the whole. Primary knowing is both deeply personal and completely communal; it is at once concretely local and wholly universal. This is why it is essential that we be wary of the pitfalls of factionalism. Primary knowing is comprehensive, whereas factionalism breaks wholes into fragments. At the same time, primary knowing is enhanced by observing reality from multiple viewpoints, for taken together they create a more comprehensive understanding.

For primary knowing to come to fruition, we have to be willing to embrace and explore ultimate questions. Primary knowing is not about superficiality. It is completely substantive; it involves the treasures of wisdom that have accumulated throughout the ages. Exploring cumulative wisdom lies at the heart of primary knowing. Wisdom develops over time. It is the fruit of the deepest of reflection on the most challenging of circumstances. Wisdom is true precisely because it has been tried. Wisdom always connects parts to whole in the most meaningful of ways. We see this in the way in which the book of Proverbs unfolds. Individual proverbs are completely concrete and relevant to specific personal concrete circumstances. And yet, in the eighth and ninth chapters, we have this wonderfully mysterious story of the creation of the world, with the mysterious woman, whose name is Wisdom, as the key, essential player in the unfolding of the cosmos. Among other things, this shows us that the fruits of wisdom are paradoxically local and universal.

Paradox and metaphor are of great assistance as we seek primary knowing. They carry our imaginations to the places where we are connected into meaningful wholes. These are places where new seeds can germinate, take root, unfold, develop, grow, and come to fruition. When Jesus says, "If any would come after me, let them deny themselves, take up their cross, and follow me; for those who would save their lives will lose them, and those who lose their lives for my sake and for the sake of the Gospel will find them," he is addressing our imaginations with paradox. Paradox is a vehicle for us to welcome, imagine, and live with—especially in the concrete circumstances that we face. The same is true for metaphor. When Jesus says, "I am the door," or "I am the vine; you are the branches," or "I am the living bread," or "I am the living water," his words carry us across a threshold into the heart of mystery. This happens as we listen, wonder, ponder, and reflect. Paradox and metaphor accomplish what propositional statements cannot do. This is because mystery is paradoxical, and we enter the heart of mystery as we are born there on the wings of metaphor.

The vision of primary knowing is what authenticates everything else. This is why Abraham built altars. He had experiences with God that were bedrock as they expanded and inflamed his imagination. Building altars, he established monuments that embodied his involvement with God and assisted in his sustaining of the mindfulness of primary knowing.

One of the mysteries of primary knowing as interconnected wholes is that primary knowing comes to fulfillment as we act on and implement the insights of primary knowing. Primary knowing involves the observation of the world leading to recognition and insight. It involves the deepest of thoughtful reflection that brings us into communion with interconnected wholes. And it comes to completion as we enact our knowing and implement our insights for the benefit of the whole. Some things seek to come into being through our own willingness and enactments.

ACKNOWLEDGMENTS

I am blessed with family members and friends who both take an interest in and help me with my writing.

I am grateful to David Hancock and the wonderful team at Morgan James Publishing for their creativity, insight, and spirit. It is a pleasure to work with such a fine production team.

I am grateful to Peter Francis, Warden of Gladstone's Library in Wales. This is a writer's paradise. The hospitality of Peter and his team is second to none.

My staff at the University of Mount Olive has shared in many of these ideas through dialogue. They are an amazing team, who greatly strengthen me with their joy and teamwork. I am delighted to thank Ashley Mitchell, Kari Sander, Emily Jenkins, Dwayne McKay, Melinda Holland, Jean Ackiss, Sharlene Howell, Nancy Westfall, Melba Ingram, Anne Hamm, Hope Fields, Mandy Hensley, Casey Heath, Rhonda Jessup, Teresa Hines, and Brenda Edwards for the honor of serving as a member of such a wonderful team.

In the same vein, I am grateful to John Williams of Cragmont Assembly, who hosted a conference of pastors and deacons where I served as keynote speaker and conference leader. This gave me the opportunity to share many of the ideas that became this book. This thoughtful group engaged in meaningful dialogue and gave me invaluable feedback.

Because I wanted to ensure that my essays are readable, I showed the first draft of this book to several trusted friends who offered me constructive feedback. They include Jim Standiford, Meriah Moore, Ryan Fields, Hope McPherson Fields, David Hines, Cheryl Hooks, and John Hill. I deeply appreciate their feedback and insight.

Mandy Hensley, artist and friend, kindly consented to paint one of the two dreams that provided connections and insight. Mandy is a gifted artist and a thoughtful human being, for whom I am grateful.

Shirley Leggett, my friend and editor, not only helps me untangle convoluted sentences, but her proofreading amazes me. I am grateful for her enthusiasm, abiding help, and support.

Choosing a person to whom to dedicate a book is both honor and pleasure. For years, Philip P. Kerstetter, President of the University of Mount Olive, has served as friend, mentor, and dialogue partner. Phil's understanding of higher education in the liberal arts tradition is second to none. I am deeply grateful for his friendship and the privilege of serving on his team.

Any insight I have into the mysteries of life are directly due to my family, I am eternally grateful to my wife Nancy, our daughter and son Jaime and Dave, and our daughter-in-law Chynnene. Conversations around the dinner table are a treasure. I cannot thank them too much.

About the Author

John N. Blackwell is Vice President for Institutional Advancement at the University of Mount Olive. For over thirty years, John has also served as speaker and retreat leader for people of all ages, both in the United States and Europe.

John received his education at San Diego State University, Claremont School of Theology, and Arizona State University, where he earned a Ph.D. in anthropology.

John and his wife, Nancy, make their home in Mount Olive, North Carolina. John enjoys reading, writing, teaching, music, travel, and kite flying.

Origin of My Birthplace is John's eighth book.

Books by John Blackwell

A Whole New World—The Gospel of Matthew: Great Insights into Transformation and Righteousness. (New York: Morgan James, 2011)

Reflections—Thoughts Worth Pondering One Moment at a Time (New York: Morgan James, 2009)

A Whole New World—the Gospel of Mark: Great Insights into Transformation and Togetherness. (New York: Morgan James, 2007)

A Whole New World—the Gospel of John: Great Insights into Transformation and Fulfillment. (New York: Morgan James, 2006)

Pride: Overcoming the First Deadly Sin (New York: Crossroad, 2006)

The Noonday Demon (New York: Crossroad, 2004)

The Passion as Story—The Gospel of Mark (Fortress Press, 1986, second printing 2010)

9 781630 471620